SOUNDS
DELICIOUS

The Flavor of Atlanta in Food & Music

from the Atlanta Symphony Orchestra — CD included

SOUNDS
DELICIOUS

The Flavor of Atlanta in Food & Music
from the Atlanta Symphony Orchestra — CD included

Published by the
Atlanta Symphony Associates

Copyright 1999 by the
Atlanta Symphony Associates
1293 Peachtree Street, NE
404-733-4839

Photography:
    Rob McDonald
Food Styling:
    Sue Strelecki and Sheridan Robinson Cupp
Atlanta Symphony Associates President:
    Sandy Cotterman
Project Chair:
    Barbara Halpern
Recipe Chair:
    Elizabeth Staples McDonald

Library of Congress Catalog Number:
    99-073458
ISBN: 0-9670854-0-3

Edited, Designed and Manufactured by
Favorite Recipes Press
an imprint of

FRP™

2451 Atrium Way
Nashville, Tennessee 37214
1-800-385-0560

Book Design: Steve Newman
Project Manager: Jane Hinshaw
Managing Editor: Mary Cummings

Manufactured in the United States of America

First Printing:
1999 12,500 copies

SPECIAL SPONSORS

Asahi Beer USA

FrontLine Concepts, Inc.

Elisa Bona Glazer and Associates

Holbrook Creative Communications

Hubbard & Associates

Rob McDonald Photography

Mednikow Jewelers

Pink Moss

PakMail of Haynes Bridge Road

Chateau Potelle

Publix

RTM Restaurant Group

Rubin Marketing Communications

Signal Graphics

Sherry Warner

Yakrus Design

PREFACE

For more than fifty years the Atlanta Symphony Associates, the volunteer organization for the Atlanta Symphony Orchestra, has shared its time, talents, and leadership in support of our Orchestra's ongoing legacy of community outreach and education. In return, we've received many times over the gift of music to delight us, move us, and broaden our horizons.

This cookbook represents the volunteer efforts of many dedicated people. The result is a collection of recipes and menus from across the Atlanta Symphony Orchestra family, and leading Atlanta restaurants and caterers, reflecting the flavor and spirit of Atlanta. In addition, Sounds Delicious features musical recordings and wine selections to enhance your dining, special stories to read from Atlanta Symphony Orchestra family members, and musical facts to discover.

Our cookbook's first edition features a special-release CD, produced exclusively for Sounds Delicious, by Telarc records and featuring the Grammy award-winning Atlanta Symphony Orchestra.

The twenty-first century presents endless possibilities and new opportunities for all of us. It is an exciting time for Atlanta and for its Orchestra. We are proud that this cookbook will be a part of your entertaining.

May all your meals blend in perfect harmony.

CONTENTS

ACKNOWLEDGEMENTS

committees

Barbara Halpern, Cookbook Chair
Sandy Cotterman, Atlanta Symphony
   Associates President
Elizabeth Staples McDonald, Recipes
Amy Rubin, Marketing
Emily Hubbard, Cookbook Launch
Caroline Coburn, Sidebars
Susan Lipsky, Sponsorship
Thelma Waldman, Administration

They were supported by
Janis Coovert, Rina Delaplane, Carla
Fackler, Al Finfer, Stephanie Fournier,
Kathy Griffin, Margaret Hall,
Ella Herlihy, Kellie Holbrook,
Mary Kitchens, Marcy Lamberson,
Lucy Lee, Donna Lewis-Walker,
Lauri Margol, Amy Mazzetta,
Cindy McGowan, Molly Mednikow,
Joanne Melcher, Leslie Schaitberger,
Kim Smith, Suzy Smith, Staci Stager,
Kaye Stanzione, Fareba Teimorabadi,
Sugie Travis, Suzy Wasserman,
Patti Wheeler, Melissa Woodard,
the Atlanta Symphony Associates
Junior Committee, and FRP.
Tony Conway, David Halpern,
Tad Lipsky, Raphael Offer,
Joe Schaitberger, and
Peter Teimorabadi
offered invaluable advice.

For the tasteful photography we owe our gratitude to Rob McDonald, who donated his time and expertise along with his wonderful imagination and ideas. Food stylist Sue Strelecki supported our efforts along with Sheridan Robinson Cupp.

Several patrons donated generously to the project: Patricia and William Brown, Sandra and Bruce Cotterman, Nancy and James Fields, Barbara and David Halpern, Lucy and Gary Lee, Susan and Tad Lipsky, Molly Mednikow, Jeanette Snee Murphy, Stacey and Raphael Offer, Doris and Rezin Pidgeon, Veronica and Alan Silverstein, Elizabeth Morgan Spiegel, and Mariette and Tom Weldon.

Raising the bar for the quality of our home entertaining were the chefs at these fine Atlanta restaurants and caterers: Affairs to Remember, Bacchanalia, Carole Parks Catering, Horseradish Grill, Legendary Events, Pano's and Paul's, and Seeger's.

Past Atlanta Symphony Associates president Lucy Lee started the ball rolling for the cookbook, and past Atlanta Symphony Associates president Carla Fackler edited copy and brought insight and order to the cookbook's components.

Nick Jones deserves far more credit than can be acknowledged here for his research on the musical selections, copy editing, and written contributions. Further appreciation goes to Rick McKelvey for support; Paul Brittan, Orchestra liaison; Atlanta Symphony Orchestra family members, who shared their stories and experiences with Caroline Coburn; George Alexsovich for coordinating our efforts in producing the **Sounds Delicious** CD; Rob Phipps and Karl Schnittke for their copy; and Jane Brigden, Meredith Harris, Clarissa Johnson, Bruce Kenney, Rachael Male, Amy Mims, Rudi Schlegel, Peter Wasserman, and Russell Williamson.

Our recipe contributors and recipe testers, who are individually recognized in a listing in the back of this book, were an invaluable part of our team and we say, "Thank you."

ABOUT THE MUSIC CD

In order to insure that all your meals blend in perfect harmony, a Compact Disk has been included in a pocket on the inside back cover of this book. It includes a selection of music chosen to complement the mood and menu for any special occasion. The music compiled on this custom CD has been recorded by the Atlanta Symphony Orchestra on the Telarc label.

Preludes — Brunches
Brahms: Scherzo from Serenade No. 1 (7:29)
Atlanta Symphony Orchestra, Yoel Levi conducting
from Telarc CD-80349, with Brahms: Variations
    on a Theme of Haydn

Intermezzo — Luncheons
Rossini: Overture to *The Barber of Seville* (7:13)
Atlanta Symphony Orchestra, Yoel Levi conducting
from Telarc CD-80334, Rossini Overtures

Intimate Interludes — Dinners for Two
Fauré: Prelude & Sicilienne from *Pelléas et Mélisande* (10:35)
Atlanta Symphony Orchestra, Robert Shaw conducting
from Telarc CD-80084, with Berlioz: Nuits d'été

Noteworthy Nights — Informal Dinners
Mendelssohn: Movement I, Symphony No. 4, "Italian" (9:15)
Atlanta Symphony Orchestra, Yoel Levi conducting
from Telarc CD-80318, with Mendelssohn: Music from
    A Midsummer Night's Dream

Great Masterpieces — Formal Dinners
Haydn: "The Heavens Are Telling" from *The Creation* (7:23)
Atlanta Symphony Orchestra and Chamber Chorus,
    Robert Shaw conducting
from Telarc CD-80298

On the Grand Scale — Cocktails and Buffets
Beethoven: Overture to *Egmont* (7:56)
Atlanta Symphony Orchestra, Yoel Levi conducting
from Telarc CD-80358, Beethoven Overtures

Outdoor Overtures — Dining al Fresco
Holst: "Jupiter" from *The Planets* (7:51)
Atlanta Symphony Orchestra, Yoel Levi conducting
from Telarc CD-80466

THE ATLANTA SYMPHONY ORCHESTRA

Since its first concerts in 1945, the Atlanta Symphony Orchestra has grown from a local youth ensemble to one of America's major orchestras. The foremost cultural organization in the southeastern United States, it serves as a cornerstone for artistic development in the region.

The Atlanta Symphony Orchestra performs more than 200 concerts each year to a combined audience estimated at more than half a million. In addition to its 72-concert main subscription season, the ASO presents light classical concerts, family concerts, an annual summer festival, outdoor summer pops concerts, free concerts in city parks, and special programs for young people, reaching more than 50,000 annually.

Recordings by the Atlanta Symphony Orchestra have drawn international praise, winning an Audio Excellence Award, *Gramophone* and *Ovation* Magazine Awards, and numerous Grammy Awards. The orchestra records for Telarc, with additional releases available on the Argo, New World, Nonesuch, Pro Arte, Sony Classical, and Vox labels.

The 95-member orchestra is complemented by the acclaimed Atlanta Symphony Orchestra Chorus of 200 voices. In 1988 the orchestra and chorus reached new levels of recognition during their European Debut Tour, performing under the baton of Robert Shaw. More than 300 musicians participated in concerts in cities from East Berlin to London. Music Director Yoel Levi led the orchestra on its second European tour in 1991, presenting sixteen concerts in fifteen cities, including London, Paris, and two concerts in Vienna. The Atlanta Symphony Orchestra was also prominently featured in the Opening Ceremonies of the Centennial Olympic Games in 1996.

Since 1993 the Atlanta Symphony Orchestra has presented annual tribute concerts to Martin Luther King, Jr. The concerts on the Morehouse College campus are broadcast internationally on National Public Radio. In 1998 the ASO launched an innovative outreach program, creating a bridge between the concert stage and the community with person-to-person partnerships.

The Atlanta Symphony Orchestra has had only three music directors in 55 years. Henry Sopkin founded the orchestra as the Atlanta Youth Symphony in 1944, presided over its transformation into a fully professional orchestra, and served as music director until 1966. Acclaimed choral and orchestral conductor Robert Shaw led the orchestra for the next 21 years, founding the Atlanta Symphony Orchestra Choruses and leading the orchestra to international fame. He held the position of Music Director Emeritus and Conductor Laureate at the time of his death in January 1999. Yoel Levi became Music Director in 1988 and is credited with shaping an orchestra now known for the clarity, virtuosity, and sonic beauty of its playing.

THE ATLANTA SYMPHONY ASSOCIATES

The Atlanta Symphony Associates is the volunteer organization for the Atlanta Symphony Orchestra and shares more than fifty years of history. Not long after the original orchestra was founded, the first volunteers were organized. Several name changes later, the Atlanta Symphony Associates is one of the nation's largest symphony support groups. In recognition of ASA's many contributions, in 1996 the principal second violin position was designated as The Atlanta Symphony Associates Chair.

Atlanta Symphony Associates has been recognized nationally for its educational efforts, receiving an American Symphony Orchestra League Sally Parker Education Award in 1996 for its role in Symphony Celebration/ A Musical Open House. One of the ASA's earliest youth education projects some forty years ago was managing the Atlanta Symphony Orchestra's Tiny Tots Concerts, believed to be among the first concerts for pre-schoolers in the nation.

Membership is open to men and women who are interested in volunteering for the orchestra. Members may also join any of nine membership units: *Allegro, Bach 'n' Rollers, Concerto, Encore, Ensemble, Fortissimo, Intermezzo, Junior Committee,* and *Supporting.* Most units meet regularly for social and musical programs.

Working together, Atlanta Symphony Associates members:

• raise more than one million dollars annually for the Atlanta Symphony Orchestra through the Decorators' Show House, Atlanta Symphony Ball, Sleighbell Luncheon and Fashion Show, Spring Garden Affair, Annual Fund Campaign, and the new Atlanta Symphony Associates cookbook, Sounds Delicious.

• bring classical music into the lives of more than 50,000 children and adults annually by presenting Music Appreciation and Meet the Artist events, ushering for children's Discovery Concerts and Symphony Street, and orchestrating Atlanta Symphony Associates outreach projects.

• show appreciation to members of the Atlanta Symphony Orchestra family by hosting Atlanta Symphony Associates Nights at the Symphony, special events for Atlanta Symphony Orchestra musicians, chorus, and staff, and the Atlanta Symphony Youth Orchestra Annual Ball.

PRELUDES
BRUNCHES

the menus

Midmorning Madrigal
Brunch Ballad
Fiesta
Bruschetta Brunch Buffet

the music

Brahms: Serenade No. 1
Variations on a Theme of Haydn
Telarc CD-80349

Prokofiev: Symphonies No. 1, "Classical," and No. 5
Telarc CD-80289

Sibelius: Finlandia and other tone poems
Telarc CD-80320

MIDMORNING MADRIGAL

creating beauty

There is no fool-proof diet for Truth, and there's no landscaped approach to Beauty. You scratch and scramble around intellectual granites; you try to understand—if not defuse or tether— your emotional tantrums; you pray for the day when your intellect and your instinct can co-exist, that the brain need not calcify the heart, or the heart o'er-flood and drown all reason.

Robert Shaw (1916–1999)
Atlanta Symphony Music Director and
   Conductor 1967–1988
Music Director Emeritus and Conductor
   Laureate 1988–1999

---

orange mimosas

CAYENNE *biscuit* WAFERS

mushroom cutlets WITH STEAMED SPINACH,
POACHED *eggs* AND HOLLANDAISE SAUCE

SOUTHERN CHEESE *grits*

FRESH *orange and grapefruit* SECTIONS

french viognier

ALMOND *blitzkuchen*

BLACKBERRY *linzertorte* COOKIES

Cayenne Biscuit Wafers

makes two dozen

ingredients

2   cups flour
1 1/2 tablespoons sugar
2   teaspoons baking powder
1   teaspoon salt
2   teaspoons cayenne pepper
1   tablespoon freshly ground
     black pepper
1/2   cup sour cream
3/4   cup heavy cream
1/4   cup melted unsalted butter

Combine the flour, sugar, baking powder, salt, cayenne and black pepper in a large bowl and mix with a fork. Mix the sour cream and heavy cream in a small bowl just until blended. Add to the dry ingredients gradually and mix lightly to form a dough; shape into a ball.

Pat into a circle on a floured surface and roll 1/2 inch thick. Cut into 2-inch circles or into desired shapes. Dip each biscuit into melted butter and place on a baking sheet lined with baking parchment or generously sprayed with nonstick cooking spray.

Bake at 425 degrees for 13 to 15 minutes or until golden brown. Serve with the Mushroom Cutlets (page 16) and steamed spinach.

Note: *For the best results, use only all-purpose flour in this recipe.*

Southern Cheese Grits

serves four

ingredients

1/2   cup quick-cooking grits
1/2   cup butter
1/2   (6-ounce) roll garlic cheese
1   egg
1/4   cup milk

Cook the grits using the package directions; cool to room temperature.

Melt the butter and cheese in a saucepan and stir to mix well; add to the grits. Beat the egg with the milk in a bowl and add to the grits; mix well.

Spoon into a greased 1-quart baking dish. Bake at 350 degrees for 30 minutes or until set.

Mushroom Cutlets

ingredients

8	ounces mushrooms, chopped
1	bunch scallions, trimmed, chopped
1	cup bread crumbs
1 1/2	cups shredded mild Cheddar cheese
2	teaspoons chopped fresh thyme
1	teaspoon salt
1	teaspoon cayenne pepper, or to taste
1	tablespoon freshly ground black pepper, or to taste
3	large eggs
2	tablespoons Worcestershire sauce
2	teaspoons Tabasco sauce, or to taste
1/4	cup sherry

Serve Mushroom Cutlets with steamed spinach and Poached Eggs (below) on Cayenne Biscuit Wafers (page 15). Top with Hollandaise sauce. For the spinach, try the recipe on page 68, omitting the garlic for faint-hearted morning people.

Combine the mushrooms, scallions, bread crumbs, cheese, thyme, salt, cayenne and black pepper in a bowl. Whisk the eggs, Worcestershire sauce, Tabasco sauce and sherry together in a small bowl. Add to the mushroom mixture and mix well with a fork. Shape into cutlets.

Sauté the cutlets in a nonstick skillet sprayed with nonstick cooking spray, turning until evenly brown on both sides. Serve immediately or hold, covered with foil, until needed; reheat in a 350-degree oven for 15 minutes or microwave on Medium for 1 1/2 minutes.

Note: *These cutlets are wonderful made into bite-sized appetizers for a buffet; they are also a good vegetarian hamburger alternative.*

Poached Eggs

ingredients

8	eggs, at room temperature
•	salt and pepper to taste

Bring 1 1/2 inches of water to a boil in a large skillet. Break the eggs 1 at a time into a custard cup and gently slide down the side of the skillet into the water. Poach for 3 to 4 minutes, agitating the skillet gently to move water.

Remove the eggs gently with a slotted spoon and season with salt and pepper. To hold, place in the refrigerator in a shallow bath of cold water and reheat briefly in a skillet of simmering water.

Mushroom Cutlets

Almond Blitzkuchen

ingredients

1	cup butter, softened
1	cup sugar
3	large egg yolks
1	tablespoon vanilla extract
1/4	teaspoon almond extract
2	cups flour, sifted
3	large egg whites
6	ounces sliced almonds
•	confectioners' sugar

Cream the butter in a mixing bowl until light. Add the sugar and beat until fluffy. Beat in the egg yolks, vanilla extract and almond extract. Add the flour and mix well.

Beat the egg whites in a mixing bowl until soft peaks form. Fold into the creamed mixture.

Spread on a greased cookie sheet. Sprinkle with the almonds and confectioners' sugar. Bake at 350 degrees for 20 minutes. Cut immediately into small squares. Cool on wire racks.

Blackberry Linzertorte Cookies makes 2 dozen

ingredients

1 1/2   cups flour
3   tablespoons cornstarch
1   tablespoon baking cocoa
1/2   teaspoon cinnamon
1/8   teaspoon nutmeg
1/8   teaspoon cloves
1/8   teaspoon salt
3/4   cup butter, softened
1/2   cup sugar
1 1/2   teaspoons grated orange peel
1   teaspoon vanilla extract
3/4   cup finely ground walnuts
1   cup blackberry jam
1/2   cup chopped walnuts

Sift the flour, cornstarch, baking cocoa, cinnamon, nutmeg, cloves and salt together in a bowl.

Cream the butter and sugar in a mixing bowl until light and fluffy. Beat in the orange peel and vanilla. Add the dry ingredients and ground walnuts gradually, mixing well after each addition.

Press into a foil-lined 9x9-inch baking pan. Pierce with a fork. Bake at 350 degrees for 40 minutes.

Melt the blackberry jam in a small saucepan over medium-low heat. Spread over the hot baked layer; sprinkle with the chopped walnuts. Bake for 15 minutes longer.

Cool in the pan on a wire rack. Cut into small bars.

for six

BRUNCH BALLAD

so much for fame

Several years ago, I was conducting the
Israel Philharmonic. On concert night I
drove into the parking lot just minutes
before the curtain, and was met by an
attendant who looked me over and said,
"Ten shekels." I gave him my name and
explained that I was conducting that
night. He listened and politely said,
"Very nice to meet you, Mr. Levi." He
then held out his hand and said, "Ten
shekels." Needless to say, I paid, and was
graciously allowed to proceed.

Yoel Levi, Atlanta Symphony Music Director
    1988–2000

MINIATURE *corn fritters*

bloody marys

LACY *green salad*

eggplant NAPOLEON

california sauvignon blanc

MILKY WAY *cake*

Miniature Corn Fritters

makes twelve

ingredients

1	tablespoon butter
2	cups fresh corn kernels
1/2	cup chopped onion
1/4	cup flour
1/2	teaspoon baking powder
1/2	teaspoon salt
1/4	teaspoon pepper
2	eggs, beaten
2	tablespoons milk
•	hot pepper sauce to taste
2	to 3 tablespoons vegetable oil

Melt the butter in a saucepan and add the corn and onion. Cook, covered, for 8 minutes; cool slightly.

Mix the flour, baking powder, salt and pepper in a mixing bowl. Add the eggs, milk and pepper sauce and mix well. Stir in the corn mixture.

Heat the oil in a skillet over medium heat. Drop the corn mixture by spoonfuls into the heated oil and flatten with a spatula. Cook until golden brown on both sides.

Lacy Green Salad

serves six

ingredients

1/2	cup vegetable oil
1/4	cup red wine vinegar or raspberry vinegar
1	teaspoon Dijon mustard
1	garlic clove, minced
•	salt and freshly ground pepper to taste
1/2	head curly endive, torn
1/2	head escarole, torn
1	head leaf lettuce, torn
•	leaves of 1/2 bunch basil

Whisk the oil, vinegar, Dijon mustard and garlic in a bowl. Season with salt and pepper.

Combine the endive, escarole, leaf lettuce and basil in a serving bowl. Add the dressing at serving time and toss to coat well.

Eggplant Napoleon

eggplant

I	large eggplant
I	tablespoon olive oil
•	salt and pepper to taste

vegetable filling

I	large shallot, finely chopped
I	zucchini, unpeeled, finely chopped
2	garlic cloves, minced
3	tablespoons olive oil
1/2	cup cream
1/2	cup bread crumbs
I	cup crumbled feta cheese
3	sprigs fresh oregano, finely chopped
•	salt and pepper to taste

onion crumb topping

I	medium onion, finely chopped
I	tablespoon olive oil
1/2	cup bread crumbs

Slice the unpeeled eggplant lengthwise into 1/4-inch slices. Brush with the olive oil and sprinkle with salt and pepper. Place on a baking sheet. Roast at 400 degrees for 15 minutes or until tender.

For the filling, sauté the shallot, zucchini and garlic in the olive oil in a skillet until tender. Reduce the heat and stir in the cream. Cook until slightly thickened, stirring frequently; remove from the heat. Add the bread crumbs, cheese, oregano, salt and pepper.

For the topping, sauté the onion in the olive oil in a skillet until tender. Add the bread crumbs and additional olive oil if needed to moisten.

To assemble, alternate layers of eggplant slices and vegetable filling in a loaf pan sprayed with nonstick cooking spray until all ingredients are used. Sprinkle the topping over the layers.

Bake at 400 degrees for 30 minutes. Let stand for 5 minutes. Invert onto a serving platter and slice to serve.

Milky Way Cake

cake

1/2   cup butter
8   regular-size Milky Way candy bars
1/2   cup butter, softened
2   cups sugar
4   eggs
1/2   teaspoon baking soda
1 1/4   cups buttermilk
3   cups flour, sifted
1   tablespoon vanilla extract

chocolate frosting

1   cup (6 ounces) semisweet chocolate chips
1/2   cup margarine
1   teaspoon vanilla extract
1   (1-pound) package confectioners' sugar, sifted twice
•   milk or cola

For the cake, melt 1/2 cup butter with the candy bars in a double boiler over low heat, stirring to blend well. Cool to room temperature.

Cream 1/2 cup butter and sugar in a mixing bowl for 5 minutes or until light and fluffy. Beat in the eggs 1 at a time.

Blend the baking soda with the buttermilk in a small bowl. Add to the creamed mixture alternately with the flour, ending with the flour and mixing well after each addition. Stir in the chocolate mixture and vanilla.

Spoon into a greased tube pan or bundt pan. Bake at 350 degrees for 1 hour or until the cake tests done. Cool in the pan for 10 minutes. Invert on the neck of a bottle to cool for 10 minutes. Tap the bottom of the pan and loosen with a knife; remove to a wire rack to cool completely.

For the frosting, melt the chocolate chips with the margarine in a double boiler. Cool for 20 minutes. Stir in the vanilla.

Add the confectioners' sugar gradually, alternately adding enough milk or cola to make of the desired consistency. Spread over the cooled cake.

for eight

FIESTA

stars and stripes forever

Exactly one year before the opening
of the 1996 Games, our orchestra's
Chastain concert had an Olympic theme,
and I had the chance to fulfill a life-long
dream of conducting. We had one
rehearsal of Sousa's "Stars and Stripes
Forever," after which I asked Yoel [Levi]
if he had any advice . . . "Yes," he said,
"when they stop playing, you stop
waving your arms!"

A. D. Frazier, Jr.
Atlanta Symphony Orchestra Board Chair
  1998–2001
[A. D. Frazier was at that time the chief
operating officer of the Atlanta Committee
for the Olympics.]

mojito

GREEN *turkey* ENCHILADAS

SPANISH *rice*

CHOPPED *cilantro salad*

white sangria

CUBAN *flan*

brownies WITH CHILES

Green Turkey Enchiladas

serves eight

green sauce

2 pounds fresh tomatillos, or
   2 (14-ounce) cans tomatillos
• water or chicken broth
6 roasted Anaheim chiles, peeled,
   seeded, or 1 (8-ounce) can whole
   green chiles
6 serrano chiles, seeded, or to taste
1 small onion
2 garlic cloves
1/2 cup chopped fresh cilantro
1/2 teaspoon sugar
2 sprigs thyme (optional)
1 teaspoon salt

enchiladas

6 cups chopped cooked
   turkey breast
2 cups sour cream
1 tablespoon dried oregano
• vegetable oil for frying
24 corn tortillas
24 ounces Monterey Jack cheese,
   shredded

For the green sauce, remove the husks from fresh tomatillos and rinse to remove stickiness. Combine with enough water or chicken broth to cover in a saucepan. Simmer for 10 minutes or until tender; drain.

Combine the tomatillos, Anaheim chiles, serrano chiles, onion, garlic, cilantro, sugar, thyme and salt in a food processor container; process until smooth. Transfer to a 5-quart saucepan and bring to a simmer.

For the enchiladas, combine the turkey with the sour cream and oregano in a large bowl and mix to coat well.

Spoon a thin layer of the green sauce into a greased shallow baking dish. Heat 1/4 inch oil in a small skillet. Arrange the tortillas, skillet, simmering sauce, a tray, the turkey mixture and the prepared baking dish as an assembly line. Dip each tortilla 1 at a time in the heated oil and fry until it begins to blister and becomes limp; do not fry until firm or crisp. Lift the tortilla, drain briefly and place in the simmering green sauce. Turn immediately in the sauce and remove to the tray.

Let tortillas stand until cool enough to handle. Spoon the turkey mixture onto the tortillas and roll to enclose the filling. Place seam side down in the baking dish. Spoon the remaining green sauce over the top.

Sprinkle with the cheese. Bake at 350 degrees for 20 minutes or just until heated through.

Note: *Use tongs with smooth edges or a single chopstick to transfer and flip the tortillas.*

Chopped Cilantro Salad

Chopped Cilantro Salad

cilantro dressing

6	tomatillos
2/3	cup lightly packed cilantro leaves
2	teaspoons chopped jalapeño pepper
2	garlic cloves
1/2	cup plus 2 tablespoons fresh lime juice
3/4	cup vegetable oil
1	cup finely chopped green onions

salad

5	cups chopped romaine lettuce
4	cups chopped green cabbage
1 1/2	cups chopped seeded tomatoes
1 1/2	cups chopped peeled jicama
1 1/2	cups fresh corn kernels
1/2	cup crumbled feta cheese
2	avocados, chopped

For the dressing, remove the husks from the tomatillos and cut into quarters. Combine with the cilantro, jalapeño pepper, garlic and lime juice in a blender container and process until puréed. Transfer to a medium bowl. Whisk in the oil and green onions. Season with salt and pepper.

For the salad, combine the romaine, cabbage, tomatoes, jicama, corn and cheese in a salad bowl and toss to mix well. Add the avocados and enough dressing to coat well; mix gently.

Serve with corn tortilla chips if desired.

Spanish Rice

ingredients

2   cups uncooked short grain rice
2   tablespoons vegetable oil
1   onion, chopped
2   fresh tomatoes, peeled, seeded, chopped
1   (8-ounce) can Mexican-style tomato sauce
3   cups water
•   salt to taste

Sauté the rice in the oil in a saucepan until light golden brown. Add the onion and tomatoes. Sauté until the rice is deep golden brown. Add the tomato sauce, water and salt.

Bring to a boil and reduce the heat. Simmer, covered, for 20 minutes or until the liquid is absorbed. Mix well before serving.

Cuban Flan

ingredients

1/2   cup sugar
5   eggs
1   (14-ounce) can sweetened condensed milk
1   (12-ounce) can evaporated milk
1   teaspoon vanilla extract

For another dessert with a Latin attitude, try Brownies with Chiles. Just add a 4-ounce can of chopped green chiles to your favorite brownie recipe or brownie mix and prepare as usual.

Sprinkle the sugar in a skillet. Cook over low heat until the sugar melts and turns golden brown, stirring frequently. Spread evenly in an 8-inch baking pan.

Combine the eggs, sweetened condensed milk, evaporated milk and vanilla in a bowl and mix well. Spoon carefully into the prepared pan. Place in a larger pan with hot water. Bake at 350 degrees for 1 hour or until a wooden pick inserted in the center comes out clean; do not allow water in larger pan to evaporate completely.

Cool the flan on a wire rack. Chill for $1^1/2$ to 2 hours. Invert onto a serving plate.

Mojito

ingredients

5   fresh mint leaves, crushed
2   teaspoons sugar
•   juice of $1/2$ lime
2   ounces light rum
•   splash of club soda
•   ice

garnish

•   mint sprig

Set up the blender in a convenient place to prepare a fresh mojito for each guest.

Combine the crushed mint leaves, sugar, lime juice, rum and club soda in a blender container. Add ice and process until smooth. Pour into a glass and garnish with a fresh mint sprig.

White Sangria

serves eight

ingredients

2   cups club soda, chilled
$1/4$ to $1/2$ cup fruit-flavored brandy
2   (750-milliliter) bottles of white wine, chilled
•   chopped fresh fruit, such as peaches, apples, pears, lemons, limes and/or berries

Combine the club soda, brandy and white wine in a large pitcher or punch bowl and mix gently. Add the fruit.

Note: *Pineapples are not recommended for this recipe.*

for twelve
BRUSCHETTA BRUNCH BUFFET

a right tricky thing

It was a busy time for the Atlanta Symphony Orchestra Board in the late 1980s. We hired a new music director, retired the former music director, made the orchestra's first European tour, and raised the funds needed for all of the above. A right tricky thing! Traveling to Europe with over 300 musicians and chorus members and accompanying instruments, sheet music, and baggage was a challenge. This was possibly the biggest musical group ever to tour from the United States—certainly from the South. In West Berlin they cleaned out every nearby store of Coke products. When the story got out, hometown Coca-Cola provided beverages for the rest of the tour!

Mary Gellerstedt
Atlanta Symphony Orchestra Board Chair
   1986–1988
Atlanta Symphony Associates President
   1982–1984

CHOCOLATE *ganache*
RASPBERRY JAM • ORANGE *marmalade*
PEANUT BUTTER
FRESH *berries* AND SLICED SEASONAL FRUIT
DRIED APRICOT HALVES • GRILLED PINEAPPLE SLICES
lentil PÂTÉ • ROASTED GARLIC AND *feta* SPREAD
FRUITED BUTTERS WITH TOASTED FRENCH BREAD SLICES

DANISH *strudel* AND FRUITED BREAKFAST *breads*

SAVANNAH *pie*

cheesecake SQUARES • CRISP *biscotti*

APPLE CRANBERRY *crisp*

coffee bar • WHIPPED CREAM • SHAVED CHOCOLATE
beringer white zinfandel
iron horse celebration cuvée sonoma county
ferrari carano chardonnay alexander valley

FROM *Affairs to Remember*

Lentil Pâté

ingredients

2   cups dried lentils
1/4   cup unsalted butter
2   cups coarsely chopped
      yellow onions
3   tablespoons brown sugar
2   tablespoons balsamic vinegar
1 1/2 cups grated carrots
1/2   teaspoon salt
1/2   teaspoon freshly ground pepper

Rinse and pick the dried lentils. Combine with water to cover in a saucepan. Cook just until tender; drain.

Melt the butter in a saucepan and add the onions. Cook, covered, over low heat until the onions are very tender. Sprinkle with the brown sugar. Cook until the mixture begins to turn golden brown. Stir in the vinegar.

Combine the lentils, onions, carrots, salt and pepper in a blender container and process until smooth. Spoon into a serving bowl.

Roasted Garlic and Feta Spread   serves twelve

ingredients

4   whole garlic bulbs
1   pound feta cheese
4   ounces cream cheese, softened
1/4   cup half-and-half
•   herbs, salt and pepper to taste

Cut off the tops of the garlic cloves, leaving the bulbs intact. Place the bulbs in a covered baking dish. Bake at 300 degrees for 1 hour. Remove the cover and bake for 20 minutes longer or until the garlic is tender and the husks are golden brown.

Squeeze the garlic cloves from the husks into a blender container. Add the feta cheese, cream cheese and half-and-half and process until smooth. Season to taste with herbs, salt and pepper.

Savannah Pie

ingredients

I	recipe (10-inch) pie pastry
I	cup shredded Swiss cheese
I	cup shredded Cheddar cheese
I	pound cooked crab meat
I	cup dry-roasted cashews
8	eggs, beaten
3	cups whipping cream
•	salt and freshly ground pepper to taste
2	tablespoons butter
$1/4$	teaspoon dried tarragon, crumbled
$1/4$	teaspoon Old Bay seasoning
$1/4$	teaspoon freshly grated nutmeg
$1/8$	teaspoon freshly ground pepper
I	large red onion, minced
$1^1/2$	(16-ounce) packages frozen chopped spinach, thawed, squeezed dry

Fit the pastry into a 10-inch springform pan and bake using the pastry recipe directions. Layer the Swiss cheese, Cheddar cheese, crab meat and cashews in the prepared crust.

Beat the eggs and cream in a mixing bowl. Season with salt and pepper to taste. Pour half the mixture over the layers, reserving the remaining portion. Place the springform pan on the center rack of an oven preheated to 450 degrees and reduce the temperature to 350 degrees. Bake for 35 to 40 minutes or until the custard portion is set but not brown.

Melt the butter in a large heavy skillet over medium-low heat. Stir in the tarragon, Old Bay seasoning, nutmeg and $1/8$ teaspoon pepper. Add the onion and cook for 10 minutes or until translucent, stirring occasionally. Add the spinach and sauté for 3 minutes.

Set aside $1/4$ cup of the reserved egg mixture. Stir the remaining egg mixture into the spinach. Spread evenly over the pie. Pour the $1/4$ cup egg mixture that was set aside over the top.

Bake for 25 to 30 minutes longer or until the custard is set and the top is golden brown. Let stand for 30 minutes. Place on a serving plate and remove the side of the pan. Cut into wedges to serve.

Chocolate Ganache

makes six cups

ingredients

1½ pounds unsalted butter
2   cups heavy cream
1¼ pounds chocolate, ground

Combine the butter and cream in a saucepan. Heat over medium heat until the butter melts, stirring to mix well. Pour the mixture into a mixing bowl.

Add the ground chocolate 1 cup at a time, beating constantly at low speed until smooth. For a light and thinner ganache, increase the amount of butter until the mixture is of the desired consistency.

Apple Cranberry Crisp

serves twelve

apple cranberry filling

6   pounds red Delicious apples, peeled, sliced
24 ounces fresh cranberries
²/₃ cup sugar
4   teaspoons ground cinnamon
2   teaspoons ground allspice
2   tablespoons orange liqueur
4   teaspoons cornstarch
2   teaspoons quick-cooking tapioca

oatmeal peanut topping

2   cups rolled oats
1   cup packed brown sugar
½   cup unsalted butter, softened
2   teaspoons ground cinnamon
½   teaspoon ground nutmeg
¾   cup roasted peanuts, finely ground

For the filling, combine the apples, cranberries, sugar, cinnamon and allspice in a heavy large saucepan over medium heat. Bring to a boil, stirring constantly. Cook for 5 minutes, stirring frequently.

Combine the liqueur, cornstarch and tapioca in a bowl and mix to dissolve the cornstarch. Stir into the fruit mixture. Reduce the heat and simmer for 2 minutes or until thickened, stirring constantly. Pour into a buttered 9x13-inch baking dish.

For the topping, mix the oats, brown sugar, butter, cinnamon, nutmeg and peanuts in a bowl until crumbly. Sprinkle over the fruit.

Bake the crisp at 350 degrees for 20 minutes or until the topping is golden brown. Cool for 10 minutes or longer. Spoon into deep dessert bowls and serve warm with vanilla ice cream.

INTERMEZZO
LUNCHEONS

the menus

Overture to Spring
Weekend Harmony
Autumn Adagio
Song of the South

the music

Rossini: Overtures
Telarc CD-80334

Kodály: Háry János/Dances of Galánta
Peacock Variations
Telarc CD-80413

Shostakovich: Symphonies No. 5 and No. 9
Telarc CD-80215

for eight
OVERTURE TO SPRING

a traveling piano

The great pianist Artur Rubinstein was guest artist with the Atlanta Symphony Orchestra in 1956 in the old Municipal Auditorium. The piano wheels had not been locked down properly, and when Rubinstein played the thundering chords that begin Tchaikovsky's First Piano Concerto, the piano began to move. Rubinstein leapt up and watched as it rolled away from him, one of its wheels dropping into the footlights. A burly French-horn player rose from his seat, single-handedly lifted the full-size concert grand out of its rut, and locked the wheels. Amused, Rubinstein joined the audience in applauding this performance, then sat down and resumed his own performance.

John Cooledge
Atlanta Symphony Orchestra Board of
    Counselors and Chorus Member

fettuccine WITH *asparagus* AND PINE NUTS

spinach SALAD

HERBED *rolls*

creamy california chardonnay

MINIATURE *coconut cakes*

FRESH *kiwifruit, papaya* AND *strawberries*

SPICED *peach tea*

Fettuccine with Asparagus and Pine Nuts

serves eight

ingredients

I	pound fresh asparagus
I	(16-ounce) package fettuccine
1/2	cup lemon juice
6	tablespoons butter
3/4	cup half-and-half
1/2	teaspoon grated lemon zest
1/3	cup grated Parmesan cheese
1/4	cup pine nuts, toasted

Trim the asparagus and peel the stalks if desired; cut into $1\frac{1}{2}$-inch pieces. Cook, covered, in a small amount of boiling water for 6 to 8 minutes or until tender-crisp; drain.

Cook the fettuccine using the package directions; drain well. Toss with the lemon juice in a large serving bowl. Let stand for I minute.

Melt the butter with the half-and-half in a small saucepan, stirring to mix well. Add to the fettuccine with the lemon peel, cheese, pine nuts and asparagus; toss gently to mix well. Serve immediately.

Spiced Peach Tea

serves eight

ingredients

6	orange-spice tea bags
3	cups boiling water
2	cups peach juice blend
I	cup water
1/4	cup sugar
2	tablespoons lemon juice
1/2	teaspoon almond extract

Steep the tea bags in the boiling water for 5 minutes, then discard the tea bags. Combine the peach juice blend, I cup water, sugar, lemon juice and almond extract in a medium saucepan and bring to a boil. Reduce the heat and simmer for 5 minutes. Combine with the tea in a pitcher and chill well. Serve over ice.

Spinach Salad

caramelized onion dressing

2   tablespoons butter
2   purple onions, sliced into rings
3   garlic cloves, minced
2   tablespoons brown sugar
3   tablespoons balsamic vinegar

salad

1   (10-ounce) package fresh spinach, torn
3   or 4 medium Roma tomatoes, chopped
•   crumbled bleu cheese (optional)

For the dressing, heat the butter in a medium skillet over medium heat until it begins to bubble. Add the onions and garlic. Sauté for 10 minutes or until the onions are golden brown. Add the brown sugar. Cook until the sugar is caramelized and thickens, stirring constantly. Stir in the vinegar. Cook for 5 minutes to blend flavors.

For the salad, spoon the hot dressing over the spinach in a large salad bowl and toss gently. Top with the tomatoes and bleu cheese.

Note: *The dressing can be made in advance and chilled. To serve, let the dressing stand until room temperature, then microwave on Medium for 2 minutes.*

Herbed Rolls

ingredients

1/2 cup margarine or butter
2 teaspoons salt
1 cup hot water
2 envelopes dry yeast
1/2 cup sugar
1 cup lukewarm water
2 eggs
5 to 6 cups bread flour
1 egg
1 tablespoon cold water
• poppy seeds, sesame seeds, herbes de provence or reconstituted dried onion flakes

Combine the margarine and salt with the hot water in a small bowl and stir to mix well. Let stand until cool. Dissolve the yeast and sugar in the warm water in a large mixing bowl. Add the margarine mixture, 2 eggs and 2 cups of the flour; mix until smooth. Add enough of the remaining flour to form a nonsticky dough.

Knead the dough on a floured surface until smooth and elastic. Place in a greased large bowl, turning to coat the surface. Let stand, covered, in a warm place until doubled in bulk. Punch down the dough and knead 5 to 10 times on a floured surface.

Divide the dough into 24 portions and roll into balls. Place in a lightly greased 9x13-inch baking pan or on a greased baking sheet. Let rise, covered, until doubled in bulk.

Beat 1 egg with 1 tablespoon cold water. Brush lightly on the rolls and sprinkle with poppy seeds. Bake at 425 degrees for 20 minutes or until golden brown.

Note: *To freeze the rolls, bake for 20 minutes or just until they begin to brown, cool completely and freeze in airtight plastic bags. To serve, bake at 350 degrees until golden brown.*

Miniature Coconut Cakes

cake

3   cups cake flour
I   tablespoon baking powder
$1/4$ teaspoon salt
$3/4$ cup unsalted butter
$1^3/4$ cups sugar
4   large egg yolks
I   tablespoon vanilla extract
I   (14-ounce) can unsweetened coconut milk
4   large egg whites
$1/4$ teaspoon cream of tartar

coconut frosting

I   (1-pound) package confectioners' sugar
$1/4$ cup unsalted butter, softened
7   ounces cream cheese
•   reserved $1/3$ cup unsweetened coconut milk
12   ounces sweetened shredded coconut

For the cake, sift the flour, baking powder and salt together. Cream the butter in a separate mixing bowl for 5 minutes or until light. Add the sugar gradually, beating constantly for 5 minutes or until fluffy. Beat in the egg yolks I at a time. Add the vanilla and mix well.

Reserve $1/3$ cup of the coconut milk. Add the dry ingredients to the batter alternately with the remaining coconut milk, ending with the dry ingredients and mixing just until blended after each addition.

Beat the egg whites with the cream of tartar in a large mixing bowl until stiff peaks form. Fold $1/2$ at a time into the batter.

Spoon into 3 buttered and parchment- or waxed-paper lined 8-inch cake pans. Bake at 350 degrees for 30 minutes or until the layers test done and the tops are puffed and golden brown; do not overbake. Cool in the pans for 20 minutes; remove to wire racks to cool completely.

For the frosting, sift the confectioners' sugar 3 times. Cream the butter and cream cheese in a mixing bowl for 5 minutes or until light and fluffy. Add the confectioners' sugar gradually, beating well after each addition. Add enough of the reserved coconut milk to achieve the desired consistency.

To assemble, cut the cake layers into small circles with a medium-large cookie cutter or biscuit cutter. Spread the frosting over the top and side of each circle. Press the coconut gently over the cakes. Serve at room temperature.

Note: *To make a 3-layer cake, spread the frosting between the 3 layers and over the top and side of the cake.*

WEEKEND HARMONY

a home run

Time: 1960s.

Place: Daytona Beach, Florida.

Event: Beethoven's 9th Symphony (London Symphony Orchestra and Atlanta Symphony Chorus, which at that time also performed with the Atlanta Symphony).

As excited chorus members, my wife Sue and I sang our best. Our son Fred, age 8, was secure (?) in an upper balcony seat. The audience stood and cheered at the glorious end of the Fourth Movement. After the concert we found our excited son in the crowd. He happily related, "I slept some and at the end I woke up with all the cheering. I thought Hank Aaron had hit another home run!" Sue and I have shared the joy of many home runs with the Atlanta Symphony and its Chorus.

Neil Williams
Atlanta Symphony Orchestra Board Chair
   1988–1990
American Symphony Orchestra League Chair
   1996–1999

hummus
WITH SNOW PEAS, CUCUMBER ROUNDS, SLICED RED BELL PEPPER AND *pita* BREAD

GRILLED *leg of lamb* WITH GRILLED *vegetables*

BAKED *sweet potato* SALAD

cabbage SALAD

spicy california cabernet sauvignon

pineapple boats WITH LEMON CURD *and berries*

Hummus

ingredients

1	(19-ounce) can chick-peas
1/2	onion
4	or 5 garlic cloves
3	tablespoons (rounded) tahini
•	juice of 1 lemon
1/4	teaspoon hot sauce
2	tablespoons soy sauce (optional)
1/2	teaspoon cumin
•	red pepper and black pepper to taste

Drain the chick-peas, reserving the liquid. Process the onion and garlic in a food processor until finely chopped. Add the chick-peas and process to a paste. Add the tahini and process until smooth.

Add the reserved chick-pea liquid gradually, processing constantly until the mixture is of the desired consistency. Add the lemon juice, hot sauce, soy sauce, cumin, red pepper and black pepper; process until smooth. Adjust the seasonings to taste.

Spoon into a serving bowl. Serve with snow peas, cucumber rounds and sliced red bell pepper.

Grilled Leg of Lamb

lamb

3   large white onions, cut into quarters

1/4   cup olive oil

5   garlic cloves, thinly sliced

•   juice of 2 lemons

2   cups plain yogurt

1   cup coarsely chopped fresh lavender or rosemary

•   freshly ground pepper to taste

1   (4 1/2- to 5-pound) leg of lamb, butterflied

grilled vegetables

•   eggplant
•   zucchini
•   sliced red bell pepper
•   olive oil and lemon juice to taste
•   salt and pepper to taste

garnish

•   lavender sprigs

For the lamb, process the onions in a food processor until puréed. Press the mixture through a sieve and measure 1 cup juice; discard the pulp.

Combine the onion juice with the olive oil, garlic, lemon juice, yogurt, chopped lavender and pepper in a nonreactive bowl and mix well. Add the lamb to the marinade, rubbing to coat well.

Marinate the lamb in the refrigerator for 5 hours or longer, turning after 3 hours. Let stand at room temperature for 1 hour before grilling.

Grill the lamb for 8 to 10 minutes on each side for medium-rare, turning every 2 or 3 minutes. Remove to a platter and let stand for 10 minutes.

For the vegetables, cut the eggplant, zucchini and bell pepper into thick slices. Drizzle with olive oil and lemon juice and season with salt and pepper. Place on the grill 5 minutes before the lamb is ready. Grill for 5 minutes or until tender-crisp.

To serve, cut the lamb into 2-inch slices. Garnish servings with sprigs of lavender. Serve with mint jelly, chutney and grilled vegetables.

Note: *Choose the shank half of the leg of lamb for a more tender cut. To prepare the lamb in the oven, bake it at 400 degrees for 30 to 35 minutes for medium-rare.*

Baked Sweet Potato Salad

curried mango chutney dressing

2   tablespoons mango chutney
1   tablespoon finely minced
    red onion
1   cup plain nonfat yogurt
1   tablespoon fresh lime juice
1½ teaspoons curry powder

salad

2½ pounds sweet potatoes
1   red bell pepper, chopped
1   cup chopped celery
¼   to ½ cup thinly sliced red onion

For the chutney dressing, combine the chutney and onion in a bowl. Add the yogurt, lime juice and curry powder and mix well. Chill in the refrigerator until needed.

For the salad, pierce the sweet potatoes several times with a fork. Bake at 400 degrees for 40 to 60 minutes or until tender. Let stand until cool enough to handle.

Combine the bell pepper, celery and onion in a large bowl. Peel and chop the sweet potatoes and add to the bowl. Add the dressing and mix gently. Serve warm or chilled.

Cabbage Salad

sweet-and-sour dressing

1¹/4 cups white wine vinegar
³/4 cup salad oil
1 cup sugar
1 tablespoon salt
1 teaspoon pepper
3 garlic cloves, crushed

salad

1 head cabbage
2 onions, thinly sliced
3 or 4 ribs of celery, chopped
2 tablespoons caraway seeds

For the dressing, combine the vinegar, oil, sugar, salt and pepper in a blender and process to mix well. Add the garlic and process until smooth.

For the salad, cut the cabbage into large squares or triangles. Combine with the onions, celery and caraway seeds in a bowl. Add the desired amount of dressing and toss to coat well.

Note: *Store any leftover dressing in an airtight container in the refrigerator.*

Pineapple Boats with Lemon Curd and Berries

serves eight

lemon curd

3/4 cup unsalted butter
1/2 cup fresh lemon juice
5 teaspoons grated lemon zest
1 teaspoon nutmeg
1 1/2 cups sugar
5 large eggs

pineapple boats

4 small pineapples
2 cups sliced strawberries
1 cup raspberries
1 cup blackberries
2 tablespoons sugar

Any combination of fresh berries will work nicely with this dish.

For the lemon curd, combine the butter, lemon juice, lemon zest and nutmeg in a heavy saucepan. Cook over medium heat until the butter melts, stirring to mix well. Bring to a boil and remove from the heat.

Whisk the sugar and eggs in a bowl. Whisk a small amount of the hot lemon mixture into the egg mixture; whisk the egg mixture into the hot lemon mixture. Cook over medium-low heat for 6 minutes or until thickened, whisking constantly; do not boil.

Pour into a clean bowl and place plastic wrap directly on the surface to prevent a skin from forming. Chill for 8 hours to 2 weeks.

For the pineapple boats, cut the pineapples into halves lengthwise. Remove the pulp and cut into bite-size pieces, discarding the cores; reserve the shells to form the boats. Wrap the shells and pulp in plastic wrap and chill for 3 hours or longer.

Combine the berries and chopped pineapple in a large bowl and toss to mix well. Spoon into the pineapple shells. Top each with 1/3 cup lemon curd; sprinkle with the sugar.

Place the boats on a baking sheet. Broil under a preheated broiler for 2 minutes or just until the sugar caramelizes and begins to brown. Serve warm.

AUTUMN ADAGIO

volunteer opportunities

Serving as Atlanta Symphony Orchestra
Board Chair offered some unique
volunteer opportunities—from cutting
the ribbon officially opening the 25th
Anniversary Decorators' Show House,
an Atlanta Symphony Associates project
that has raised two million dollars
over the years, to acting as master of
ceremonies for two Symphony Balls, the
latter featuring three events attended by
1,100 celebrants. The 1995 Symphony
Ball honored Alene Uhry, who has been
a symphony volunteer for more than
50 years and a Board member for many
years. Before going on stage for her
introduction, Alene turned to those
assembled and remarked, "Most ladies
my age aren't buying new ball gowns."

John Glover
Atlanta Symphony Orchestra Board Chair
   1994–1996

CORN AND PUMPKIN *chowder*

OPEN-FACE *meat loaf sandwiches* WITH
OVEN-ROASTED *tomatoes,*
CRISP GREEN LEAF LETTUCES, CHUTNEY, AND
MARINATED *jalapeño* PEPPERS

australian shiraz
chilled microbrew beers

CINNAMON RAISIN OATMEAL *cookies*

hot wassail

Meat Loaf

ingredients

1	large yellow onion, chopped
8	ounces lean ground beef
8	ounces ground veal
8	ounces ground pork, chicken or chorizo
1	bunch scallions, chopped
4	garlic cloves, chopped
$1/2$	cup catsup
$1/4$	cup horseradish
3	tablespoons Worcestershire sauce
•	Tabasco sauce to taste
1	teaspoon dry mustard
2	teaspoons dried oregano
•	salt and pepper to taste
2	eggs, lightly beaten
$3/4$	cup bread crumbs
$1/4$	cup catsup
1	tablespoon brown sugar

This versatile combination can also be browned and added to your favorite marinara sauce for a delicious pasta accompaniment.

Sauté the onion in a nonstick skillet until tender. Combine with the ground beef, ground veal, ground pork, scallions, garlic, $1/2$ cup catsup, horseradish, Worcestershire sauce, Tabasco sauce, dry mustard, oregano, salt and pepper in a bowl and mix well with the hands. Add the eggs and bread crumbs and mix well.

Press into a 4x8-inch baking pan. Mix $1/4$ cup catsup with the brown sugar in a small bowl. Spread over the top of the meat loaf. Bake at 350 degrees for $1^{1}/4$ hours. Let stand for several minutes and remove to a platter. Slice to serve.

For sandwiches, let the meat loaf stand until cool enough to slice easily. Serve open-face on baguette rounds with roasted red peppers or Oven-Roasted Tomatoes (page 52).

Corn and Pumpkin Chowder

Corn and Pumpkin Chowder

pesto

3/4 cup fresh cilantro leaves
I cup fresh parsley leaves
1/2 cup pine nuts, lightly toasted
1/2 cup grated Parmesan cheese
2 medium garlic cloves, minced
2 jalapeño peppers, chopped
1 1/2 tablespoons fresh lime juice
3/4 teaspoon grated lime zest
1/2 cup (about) olive oil

chowder

1 1/2 medium red bell peppers
3/4 cup chopped yellow onion
1 1/2 tablespoons olive oil
3 tablespoons finely chopped jalapeño pepper
4 (14-ounce) cans chicken stock
2 (11-ounce) niblets corn
I (24-ounce) can pumpkin
I tablespoon cumin
I tablespoon ground chipotle pepper
• salt and black pepper to taste
6 large flour tortillas
6 tablespoons half-and-half

Break off pieces of the tortilla bowls and dip them into this delicious chowder as you eat.

For the pesto, combine the cilantro, parsley, pine nuts, cheese and garlic in a food processor container. Process for 10 to 15 seconds or until chopped. Add the jalapeño peppers, lime juice and lime zest and process until smooth. Add the olive oil gradually, processing constantly until smooth.

For the chowder, place the bell peppers on a baking sheet. Broil until charred on all sides, turning often. Place in a large bowl and cover with plastic wrap; let stand until skins peel off easily. Discard skins and chop the peppers.

Sauté the onion in the olive oil in a large saucepan over low heat. Add the roasted pepper and jalapeño pepper and sauté until the onion is translucent. Add the chicken stock and corn. Bring to a boil and add the pumpkin, cumin, ground chipotle pepper, salt and black pepper. Cook until heated through.

Cut the tortillas into halves and place 2 halves in each of six ovenproof serving bowls. Bake at 350 degrees for 15 minutes or until golden brown.

Stir the half-and-half into the soup. Ladle into the prepared bowls. Top each serving with a dollop of the pesto.

Oven-Roasted Tomatoes

serves six

ingredients

1/4   cup olive oil
1   small yellow onion, chopped
2   garlic cloves, sliced
1   sprig fresh rosemary, chopped
3   tablespoons chopped fresh parsley
6   large ripe plum tomatoes,
     quarters, or 1 can plum tomatoes,
     drained, chopped
2   teaspoons balsamic vinegar
1/2   tablespoon sugar
•   salt and pepper to taste

To achieve the best flavor with these tomatoes, they should be roasted in a 250-degree oven for about 3 hours. However, the following recipe can be made in about 20 minutes with almost the same results.

Drizzle half the olive oil over the bottom of a roasting pan. Add the onion, garlic, rosemary and parsley and toss to coat well. Add the tomatoes and drizzle with the remaining olive oil and vinegar. Sprinkle with the sugar, salt and pepper.

Roast at 475 degrees for 20 minutes. Broil for about 5 minutes longer, watching carefully to prevent burning. Serve on the open-face Meat Loaf Sandwiches (page 49) or other sandwiches.

Note: *These may also be served with grilled meats and seafood, or in salads, pastas or vinaigrettes.*

Marinated Jalapeño Peppers

makes one pint

ingredients

2   cups sliced seeded fresh or canned
     jalapeño peppers
1   cup plus 2 tablespoons vinegar
1/2   cup sugar
1   tablespoon whole cloves

Combine the peppers with the vinegar in a 1-pint jar. Marinate, covered, in the refrigerator for 3 days. Drain the peppers, reserving 3/4 cup of the vinegar. Combine the reserved vinegar with the sugar, stirring to partially dissolve. Add to the peppers with the cloves. Marinate for 24 hours longer.

Cinnamon Raisin Oatmeal Cookies

makes two dozen

ingredients

1 1/2 cups flour
1 teaspoon baking soda
2 cups quick-cooking oats
1 teaspoon cinnamon
1/2 teaspoon nutmeg
1 teaspoon salt
1 cup raisins
1 cup butter or shortening, softened
1 cup packed brown sugar
1/2 cup sugar
2 tablespoons milk
2 eggs
1 1/2 teaspoons vanilla extract
1 cup broken pecans or walnuts

Mix the flour, baking soda, oats, cinnamon, nutmeg and salt together. Combine the raisins with hot water to cover in a bowl and let stand to plump; drain.

Cream the butter, brown sugar and sugar in a mixing bowl until light and fluffy. Add the milk, eggs and vanilla and mix at low speed just until blended.

Add the dry ingredients and beat at low speed until well mixed, scraping the bowl frequently. Stir in the raisins and pecans.

Drop by rounded tablespoonfuls 3 inches apart on an ungreased cookie sheet. Bake at 375 degrees for 15 minutes or until light brown. Remove immediately to a wire rack to cool. Store in an airtight container.

Wassail

makes ten cups

ingredients

2 quarts apple juice
2 cups cranberry juice
1/2 cup sugar
2 cinnamon sticks
1 teaspoon whole allspice
1 teaspoon aromatic bitters
1 small orange studded with whole cloves
1 cup dark rum

Combine the apple juice, cranberry juice, sugar, cinnamon, allspice, bitters and orange in a large saucepan. Cook over medium to high heat for 1 hour. Reduce the heat and simmer for 3 to 4 hours. Add the rum just before serving.

SONG OF THE SOUTH

moving along

At the old Municipal Auditorium, the floor boards seemed to squeak each time Mr. Sopkin and the orchestra reached a particularly melodious part of the program. And, you could always tell when the symphony followed the circus. You can't imagine the joy and excitement when the Arts Center opened in 1968 and we had our very own Symphony Hall. The orchestra even had a rehearsal hall, following years of rehearsing in schools, church basements, and, one year, the Atlanta Braves locker room. Thirty years later, we can now dream of a new great hall equal to our even greater orchestra.

Betty Fuller
Atlanta Symphony Orchestra Board Chair
   1977–1979
Atlanta Symphony Associates President
   1972–1973

shrimp jumbo WITH GRITS

sea bass WITH BUTTERNUT SQUASH RAGOUT

BRAISED *collard greens*

ferrari carano fumé blanc

KENTUCKY OATMEAL *spice cake*

FROM *Horseradish Grill*

Shrimp Jumbo with Grits

serves four

cheesy grits

2 cups Logan Turnpike
    stone-ground grits
•   cold water
4   cups milk
2   cups water
$1/2$ cup butter
$1/2$ cup cream
$1/2$ cup grated Parmesan cheese
•   salt and pepper to taste

shrimp

3   red bell peppers
2   large onions, cut into strips
2   tablespoons butter
20   large shrimp, peeled, deveined
2   tablespoons olive oil
1   teaspoon chopped garlic
•   red pepper flakes to taste
2   tablespoons chopped
    Italian parsley
1   cup sherry
2   tablespoons butter
•   salt and pepper to taste

For the grits, combine the grits with enough cold water to cover them in a bowl and skim the pith that floats to the surface; pour off the water. Combine the grits with the milk and 2 cups water in a noncorrosive saucepan. Cook over low heat for 3 to 4 hours or until thickened, stirring every 15 minutes. Add the butter, cream, cheese, salt and pepper and mix well.

For the shrimp, grill the bell peppers until the skins begin to char, turning to char evenly. Place in a bowl and cover with plastic wrap; let stand for 15 minutes. Remove the skins and seeds and cut the peppers into strips.

Sauté the onions in 2 tablespoons butter in a skillet over high heat until browned.

Sauté the shrimp in the olive oil in a large sauté pan over high heat just until translucent. Remove the shrimp with a slotted spoon. Add the garlic, sautéed onions, roasted peppers, pepper flakes and parsley. Cook for 3 minutes, stirring constantly.

Stir in the sherry and bring to a boil. Cook until reduced by $1/4$. Add the shrimp and 2 tablespoons butter and stir to coat well. Season with salt and pepper.

To serve, spoon the grits onto the serving plates. Spoon the shrimp mixture over the grits.

Sea Bass with Butternut Squash Ragout and Braised Collard Greens

serves four

braised collard greens

2   pounds ham hocks or
     country ham
I   gallon water
4   to 5 pounds collard greens

butternut squash ragout

4   to 5 pounds butternut squash
3   tablespoons butter
I   teaspoon salt
$1/4$ teaspoon pepper
I   tablespoon butter
2   cups cream
3   tablespoons honey
I   teaspoon allspice
I   teaspoon nutmeg
$1/2$ teaspoon cinnamon
$1/2$ teaspoon salt

sea bass

2   tablespoons olive oil
4   (7- to 8-ounce) portions of
     sea bass
•   salt and pepper to taste

For the collard greens, simmer the ham hocks in the water in a covered stockpot for 3 hours. Remove the ham hocks and add the collard greens in batches. Cook for 30 to 45 minutes or until tender.

For the ragout, peel the squash and cut into halves, discarding the seeds. Cut the squash into $1/2$-inch cubes. Reserve about $1^1/2$ pounds of the cubes. Melt 3 tablespoons butter in a saucepan. Add the remaining squash, I teaspoon salt and pepper, mixing gently to coat well. Spread on a baking sheet. Roast at 400 degrees until squash is tender and golden brown.

Sauté the reserved squash in I tablespoon butter in the saucepan for 10 minutes. Add the cream, honey, allspice, nutmeg, cinnamon and $1/2$ teaspoon salt. Simmer for 30 to 45 minutes or until the squash is very tender. Process the mixture in a food processor or blender until smooth.

Combine the roasted squash and puréed squash in the saucepan and mix gently. Cook just until heated through.

For the sea bass, heat the olive oil in a nonstick sauté pan over medium-high heat. Sprinkle the fish with salt and pepper and add to the sauté pan. Sauté on I side for 3 to 4 minutes or until lightly browned.

Turn the fish over and place the pan in a 400-degree oven. Bake for 5 minutes or until the fish flakes easily. Serve with the butternut squash ragout and braised collard greens.

Kentucky Oatmeal Spice Cake serves twelve

cake

1 1/2   cups flour
1   teaspoon baking soda
1/4   teaspoon nutmeg
1/2   teaspoon cinnamon
1/2   teaspoon salt
1 1/4   cups boiling water
1   cup rolled oats
1/2   cup unsalted butter, softened
1   cup sugar
1   cup packed light brown sugar
2   eggs, at room temperature
1   teaspoon vanilla extract

coconut-pecan topping

1/4   cup unsalted butter, softened
1   cup packed light brown sugar
1/2   cup heavy cream
1   cup chopped pecans
1   cup sweetened flaked coconut

For the cake, sift the flour, baking soda, nutmeg, cinnamon and salt together and set aside. Pour the boiling water over the oats in a small bowl and mix well. Let stand for 15 minutes.

Cream the butter, sugar and brown sugar in a mixing bowl until light and fluffy. Beat in the eggs and vanilla. Add the dry ingredients gradually, beating constantly at low speed and scraping the side of the bowl frequently. Mix in the oats.

Spread in a greased and floured 9x13-inch cake pan. Bake at 350 degrees for 25 minutes or until a wooden pick inserted into the center comes out clean. Cool in the pan on a wire rack.

For the topping, mix the butter and brown sugar by hand in a medium bowl. Blend in the cream. Add the pecans and coconut and mix well.

Spread over the cake. Broil just until the topping is golden brown.

INTIMATE INTERLUDES
DINNERS FOR TWO

the menus

Tango for Two
Italian Infatuation
Romantic Duet
Dolce Valentine

the music

Fauré: *Pelléas et Mélisande*
Telarc CD-80084

Brahms: Alto Rhapsody and Choral Works
Telarc CD-80176

Fauré and Duruflé: Requiems
Telarc CD-80135

Tchaikovsky: Piano Concerto No. 1
Saint-Saëns: Piano Concerto No. 2
Telarc CD-80386

TANGO FOR TWO

"elijah" speaks

I first met Yoel Levi when he was called in at the last minute for his first *Elijah* with the San Francisco Symphony and as a replacement for Robert Shaw. In the Shaw version for that performance, the chorale, "Cast Thy Burden Upon the Lord," was not being performed. During rehearsal with Maestro Levi, after performing the aria which directly precedes the chorale, I told him that if he ever performed *Elijah* again to be sure and include the chorale. Not only is it exceptionally beautiful, it also ends with a musical quote from the aria that completes the musical idea. Yoel reached for a pencil and began scribbling something across the top of the score that I couldn't read. When I asked, "What language is that?" he replied, "Elijah's!"

William Stone, Baritone
Frequent Atlanta Symphony Guest Soloist

caviar WITH TOAST POINTS

MARINATED *walnut* SALAD

seafood pasta BAKED IN PARCHMENT

french burgundy

raspberries IN CHOCOLATE GANACHE

french champagne

Marinated Walnut Salad

marinated walnut dressing

$1^1/2$ teaspoons cider vinegar
$2^1/4$ teaspoons fresh lemon juice
$^3/4$ teaspoon finely chopped fresh dill
$^3/4$ teaspoon finely chopped
 fresh mint
$^3/4$ teaspoon finely chopped
 fresh parsley
• salt and pepper to taste
3 tablespoons olive oil
$^1/4$ cup chopped walnuts

salad

1 bunch frizée
1 bunch watercress
1 (6-ounce) jar artichoke hearts
 or marinated artichoke
 hearts, chopped
$^1/4$ cup finely sliced apple

For the dressing, combine the vinegar, lemon juice, dill, mint, parsley, salt and pepper in a medium bowl. Add the olive oil gradually, stirring constantly to mix well. Stir in the walnuts. Marinate, covered, in the refrigerator for 1 to 2 days.

For the salad, arrange the lettuce leaves and watercress on the serving plates. Top with the artichokes and apple. Drizzle with the dressing.

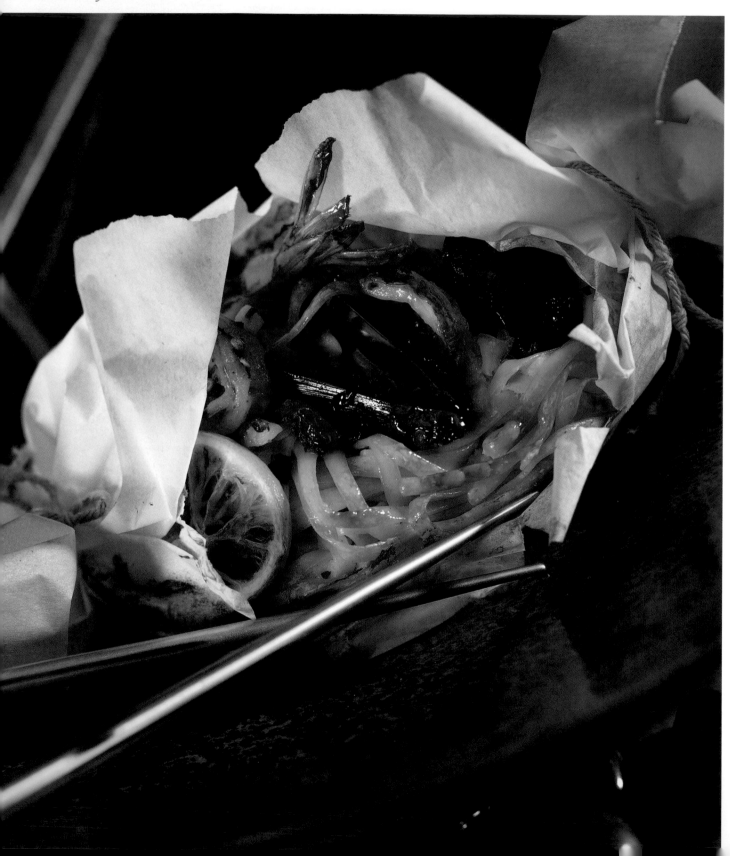

Seafood Pasta Baked in Parchment

serves two

ingredients

8	ounces mussels
4	ounces uncooked shrimp
2	whole uncooked lobster tails
8	ounces uncooked fettuccine
3	tablespoons finely chopped shallots
3	tablespoons finely chopped garlic
I	tablespoon chopped parsley
1/4	teaspoon red pepper flakes
•	salt to taste
I	teaspoon black pepper
1/4	cup olive oil
1/2	cup chopped tomato
1/2	cup bottled clam juice
1/2	cup white wine
1/4	cup chopped fresh basil
I	lemon, thinly sliced
1/4	cup grated Parmesan cheese

Line 2 small ovenproof dishes with large sheets of baking parchment, allowing enough to fold over the top. Scrub the mussels, discarding any that are not firmly closed. Peel the shrimp. Remove the meat from the lobster tails and cut into strips.

Cook the fettuccine al dente using the package directions. Drain and place in the prepared dishes.

Sauté the shallots, garlic and parsley with the red pepper flakes, salt and black pepper in the olive oil in a large sauté pan for 2 minutes. Add the tomato and sauté for 4 minutes or until the tomato is tender.

Add the clam juice, wine and basil and bring to a simmer. Add the seafood and cook briefly; seafood will continue to cook in the oven. Spoon the seafood and cooking liquid over the pasta in the prepared dishes. Arrange the lemon slices around the inner edges.

Fold the parchment to enclose the seafood and pasta, making a tight seal but leaving air in the bundle to steam the food; tie with string.

Bake at 450 degrees for 12 to 15 minutes. Remove the bundles gently and place on individual plates or a serving platter. Cut the bundles open at the table and serve directly from the parchment. Sprinkle with the cheese.

Raspberries in Chocolate Ganache

Raspberries in Chocolate Ganache

chocolate ganache

3   ounces chocolate bar or
    chocolate chips
1/3 cup heavy cream

raspberry filling

1   pint raspberries
2   tablespoons sugar
2   tablespoons plus 2 teaspoons
    fresh orange juice
1/2 teaspoon fresh lemon juice
1 1/2 teaspoons raspberry liqueur

For the ganache, chop the chocolate and place in a small bowl. Heat the cream until hot but not boiling in a small saucepan. Pour over the chocolate and let stand for 4 minutes. Stir quickly with a spoon until the mixture becomes very smooth and velvety.

Spoon several tablespoonfuls into each of 2 stemmed dishes or glasses, turning the dish to coat the side evenly. Place in the freezer until set. Repeat the process if necessary to coat evenly. Freeze until serving time.

For the filling, reserve half the raspberries. Combine the remaining raspberries with the sugar, orange juice, lemon juice and liqueur in a bowl or blender container. Process with a hand blender or standing blender until puréed. Press through a fine sieve into a bowl. Chill, covered, until serving time or for up to 3 days.

To assemble, place the reserved raspberries in the chocolate-coated dishes. Spoon the raspberry purée over the top. Serve immediately.

Note: *You may fill the chocolate-coated dishes with vanilla ice cream and spoon the raspberry purée over the top if preferred.*

ITALIAN INFATUATION

corn-fed hospitality

While on tour in the early 1970s, the Atlanta Symphony Orchestra was on its way to Decorah, Iowa, in a caravan of three Greyhound buses. Traveling a state road with few farms, little traffic, and deep snow, the lead bus overheated. The driver lurched through the snow and by repeatedly turning on the ignition switch, he literally jumped the bus into a farmyard. When the three buses appeared, the surprised farmer and his wife offered to feed the nearly one hundred stranded musicians! While the driver plugged the leaking hole in the radiator, the musicians staged a snowball fight and a tour of the livestock barn.

Martin Sauser
Atlanta Symphony Orchestra Concertmaster
    1957–1974

STEAMED ARTICHOKES WITH *aïoli*

pinot blanc

veal PICCATA

BAKED PARMESAN *polenta*

LEMON-GARLIC *spinach*

italian sangiovese

CLASSIC *tiramisu*

Aïoli

ingredients

1	garlic clove, minced
1	cup olive oil
2	egg yolks
1	teaspoon Dijon mustard
1	tablespoon lemon juice
1	garlic clove, minced
1	tablespoon grated lemon zest
1	teaspoon salt
•	pepper to taste

Sauté 1 garlic clove in $^1/_4$ cup of the olive oil in a skillet over low heat for 1 minute; do not brown. Cool garlic oil to room temperature. Mix the egg yolks and Dijon mustard in a bowl and whisk in the remaining $^3/_4$ cup olive oil very gradually. Whisk in the lemon juice, 1 garlic clove, lemon zest, salt, pepper and garlic oil.

Serve with steamed artichokes, zucchini, as a dip with crudités, on sandwiches or with fried fish.

Veal Piccata

ingredients

2	veal cutlets
3	tablespoons unbleached flour
$^1/_2$	tablespoon (or more) butter
1	tablespoon (or more) olive oil
1	large garlic clove, minced
1	shallot, minced
1	tablespoon lemon juice
$^1/_4$	cup dry white wine
1	tablespoon capers with liquid

Pound the veal cutlets very thin between waxed paper with a meat mallet. Coat with the flour.

Melt the butter with the olive oil in a skillet over medium-low heat and heat until the butter sizzles. Add the garlic and shallot. Sauté until golden brown.

Add the veal to the skillet and sauté until golden brown on both sides, adding additional butter or olive oil as needed; garlic may become very dark. Remove the veal to a plate.

Add the lemon juice, wine and capers to the skillet, stirring to deglaze. Cook over medium heat for 5 minutes or until the sauce thickens slightly.

Return the veal to the skillet and spoon the sauce over the tops. Cook just until heated through and serve immediately.

Note: *Chicken breasts or cutlets or turkey cutlets may be substituted for the veal in this recipe.*

Baked Parmesan Polenta

serves two

ingredients

1 1/4 cups plus 2 tablespoons reduced-
        sodium chicken broth
1   cup water
3/4   cup milk
1 1/2 garlic cloves, minced
3/4   teaspoon chopped fresh rosemary
1/4   teaspoon salt
3/4   cup coarse yellow cornmeal
3   tablespoons grated
        Parmesan cheese
•   pepper to taste
1   tablespoon grated
        Parmesan cheese

Combine the chicken broth, water, milk, garlic, rosemary and salt in a heavy medium saucepan and bring to a boil. Add the cornmeal very gradually, whisking constantly until smooth.

Reduce the heat and simmer for 12 minutes or until the mixture is thick and creamy, stirring occasionally. Remove from the heat and stir in 3 tablespoons cheese. Season with pepper.

Spoon into a 1-quart baking dish that has been buttered or sprayed with nonstick cooking spray. Sprinkle with 1 tablespoon cheese. Bake at 375 degrees for 30 minutes or until heated through and golden brown.

Note: *This dish may be prepared a day in advance, cooled and chilled, covered, until baking time.*

Lemon-Garlic Spinach

serves two

ingredients

2   garlic cloves, chopped
•   olive oil
1   bunch spinach
1   tablespoon lemon juice
•   salt and pepper to taste

Sauté the garlic in a small amount of olive oil in a saucepan over low heat. Add the spinach and sauté until the liquid evaporates. Season with the lemon juice, salt and pepper.

Classic Tiramisu

ingredients

1	cup whipping cream
2	teaspoons vanilla extract
3	egg yolks
$1/4$	cup sugar
4	ounces cream cheese, softened
8	ounces mascarpone cheese, softened
$1/3$	cup marsala
2	cups warm espresso or strong coffee
1	cup marsala
2	tablespoons sugar
3	packages ladyfingers
3	tablespoons baking cocoa

Beat the whipping cream with the vanilla in a mixing bowl until soft peaks form.

Beat the egg yolks with $1/4$ cup sugar at high speed in a mixing bowl until thick and pale yellow. Add the cream cheese and beat at medium speed until smooth. Add the mascarpone cheese and $1/3$ cup wine and mix until blended. Fold in half the whipped cream. Chill in the refrigerator.

Mix the espresso, 1 cup wine and 2 tablespoons sugar in a bowl. Dip the ladyfingers in the espresso mixture and arrange 1 layer over the bottom and side of a trifle bowl or other glass dish.

Layer with half the cheese mixture and remaining whipped cream, dusting the whipped cream with half the baking cocoa. Repeat the layers. Chill for 8 hours or longer before serving.

ROMANTIC DUET

applause to remember

The 1988 performance in East Berlin
of the Beethoven 9th Symphony was
an incredible experience. At the end,
the applause went on and on. Mr. Shaw
kept coming out and bowing, and
finally he dragged off the Concertmaster.
The audience continued to applaud.
Eventually, everyone on stage was gone—
the conductor, the soloists, and the
orchestra. I was one of the last to leave
the stage, and the audience showed no
sign of stopping. It still moves me to
remember it, and I hope they're still over
there clapping!

Steven Reed, Symphony Chorus Member

LOBSTER AND TOMATO *bisque*

fillet of beef WITH MERLOT SAUCE

HERBED MASHED *potatoes*

baby carrots WITH HORSERADISH BUTTER

STEAMED *snow peas*

vintage bordeaux

CHOCOLATE *truffles*

vintage port

Lobster and Tomato Bisque

ingredients

1/2	cup chopped yellow onion
1	shallot, minced
1/2	cup finely chopped celery
2	teaspoons butter
1/2	recipe Oven-Roasted Tomatoes (page 52)
1	(5-ounce) can evaporated milk
3/4	cup chicken broth
1/2	teaspoon Old Bay seasoning
•	Tabasco sauce, salt and pepper to taste
4	ounces cooked lobster, chopped

garnish

2	fresh basil leaves or tarragon sprigs

Sauté the onion, shallot and celery in the butter in a saucepan until tender. Process in a food processor until smooth. Add the roasted tomatoes and process until nearly smooth, allowing some chunks to remain. Return to the saucepan.

Add the evaporated milk and chicken broth. Bring to a slow boil over medium heat and immediately reduce the heat to low. Simmer for 20 minutes; do not boil.

Add the Old Bay seasoning, Tabasco sauce, salt and pepper. Stir in half the lobster. Place the remaining lobster in 2 soup bowls and ladle the soup into the bowls. Garnish with basil or tarragon.

Lobster and Tomato Bisque on page 71

Fillet of Beef with Merlot Sauce

serves two

ingredients

1/2   cup beef broth
1/4   cup merlot or other dry red wine
1   teaspoon seedless raspberry jam
1/4   teaspoon pepper
2   thin (1-ounce) slices pancetta
2   (6- to 8-ounce) beef fillet steaks,
      about 1 1/2 inches thick
•   salt to taste

Combine the beef broth, wine, raspberry jam and pepper in a 1- to 2-quart saucepan. Bring to a boil over high heat and cook for 7 minutes or until reduced to 1/2 cup.

Wrap 1 slice of pancetta around the edge of each steak. Place on a rack in a broiling pan. Broil 4 to 6 inches from the heat source for 6 to 7 minutes on each side for rare or until done to taste.

Place the steaks on warm plates and spoon the merlot sauce over the tops. Season with salt.

Note: *Pancetta is sold in well-stocked supermarkets and Italian delis.*

for two
DOLCE VALENTINE

timing is everything

The 1991 Atlanta Symphony Orchestra's European tour was in grave danger of being cancelled because of funding. First, the Atlanta Symphony Associates stepped in with a significant amount from its reserve fund (an Atlanta Symphony Associates Chair was named for this heroic effort) and, then, luck came upon us. Delta Air Lines announced they would acquire Pan Am Airways! The Delta name—well-known nationally—was not so well-known in Europe, so visibility was important. Delta made the wonderful decision to become presenting sponsor and the tour went forward. It was spectacularly successful, with rave reviews and standing ovations in London, Paris, and each of the cities visited, with a sincere invitation to return again.

Jay Levine
Atlanta Symphony Orchestra Board Chair
1990–1992

POTATO *crab* CAKE *salad*

young california sauvignon blanc OR *pinot gris*

HERB-CRUSTED RACK OF *lamb with caponata*

big spicy california merlot

CARAMELIZED *coconut crème* WITH MANGO LIME

FROM *Pano's and Paul's*

Potato Crab Cake Salad

crab cakes

12	ounces Yukon gold potatoes
6	ounces lump crab meat
1/2	beaten egg
1/2	tablespoon mayonnaise
1/2	tablespoon flour
•	juice of 1/4 lemon
1/4	teaspoon minced fresh tarragon
•	Old Bay seasoning, salt and pepper to taste
•	olive oil or butter

salad

1	tablespoon sherry vinegar
1 1/4	tablespoons olive oil
•	salt and freshly ground white pepper to taste
2	ounces mesclun or mixed lettuces

For the crab cakes, partially cook the unpeeled potatoes in water to cover in a saucepan; do not cook until tender. Drain, cool and peel the potatoes. Shred with a large shredder.

Pick the crab meat and pat dry, discarding any shell. Combine with the potatoes, egg, mayonnaise, flour, lemon juice, tarragon, Old Bay seasoning, salt and pepper in a bowl and mix well.

Shape the crab mixture as desired. Coat with additional flour if a drier consistency is desired. Sauté in a small amount of olive oil or butter until golden brown.

For the salad, combine the vinegar, olive oil, salt and white pepper in a covered jar and shake to mix well. Place the mesclun or mixed lettuces on salad plates; drizzle with the vinaigrette. Arrange the crab cakes beside the salad.

Herb-Crusted Rack of Lamb with Caponata

serves two

caponata

2	cups chopped eggplant
1	cup chopped zucchini
1	cup chopped red bell pepper
$1/2$	cup chopped celery
•	olive oil
$1/2$	cup chopped onion
$1/2$	tablespoon sugar
2	tablespoons red wine vinegar
1	cup tomato sauce
2	tablespoons sliced black olives
$1/2$	tablespoon capers
$1/2$	tablespoon each minced parsley and oregano
•	red pepper flakes, salt and black pepper to taste
$1/2$	tablespoon pine nuts
$1/2$	tablespoon raisins

lamb

1	(8-bone) French-cut rack of lamb
•	salt and pepper to taste
•	olive oil
$1/2$	cup bread crumbs
$1/2$	tablespoon flour
2	tablespoons chopped fresh basil
$1/2$	tablespoon fresh rosemary leaves
2	tablespoons Dijon mustard

garnish

•	fresh herbs

For the caponata, sauté the eggplant, zucchini, bell pepper and celery separately in olive oil in a heavy sauté pan, cooking each until tender and light brown and removing to a baking sheet to cool.

Sauté the onion in olive oil in the sauté pan until tender and light brown. Sprinkle with the sugar and cook until golden brown. Add the vinegar and simmer for 1 minute.

Stir in the tomato sauce, olives and capers and cook until the mixture is reduced and thickened. Add the parsley, oregano, red pepper flakes, salt and black pepper.

Combine with the eggplant mixture, pine nuts and raisins in a bowl and mix well. Let stand until cool.

For the lamb, season the lamb with salt and pepper. Brush with olive oil. Sear in a nonstick skillet or grill just long enough to seal in the juices. Remove to a rack in a broiling pan. Broil for 15 to 20 minutes for medium-rare. Let stand for several minutes.

Combine the bread crumbs, flour, basil and rosemary in a bowl and mix well. Brush the lamb with the Dijon mustard and press the bread crumb mixture over the surface. Roast until the crust is golden brown and the lamb is done to taste.

To serve, cut the lamb into single chops. Place the caponata on the serving plates and top with the chops. Garnish with additional fresh herbs.

Note: *The caponata can be made ahead of time. It can be served warm or at room temperature for sandwiches or as a side dish.*

Caramelized Coconut Crème with Mango Lime

serves two

ingredients

2   tablespoons sugar
2   eggs
2   tablespoons sugar
1/4 cup milk
2/3 cup coconut milk
•   seeds of 1/2 vanilla bean, or
     1 teaspoon vanilla extract
1   ripe mango, chopped
•   lime juice and sugar to taste

garnish

•   raspberries
•   confectioners' sugar

Spray 2 ramekins with nonstick cooking spray. Sprinkle 2 tablespoons sugar in a small saucepan. Cook over medium-high heat until the sugar melts and turns golden brown, shaking the saucepan constantly. Pour immediately into the prepared ramekins and swirl to coat evenly. Place in a baking pan filled with 1/2 inch water.

Whisk the eggs with 2 tablespoons sugar in a bowl. Add the milk, coconut milk and vanilla bean seeds and whisk to mix well. Pour into the prepared ramekins. Cover the pan tightly with foil.

Bake the custards at 300 degrees for 45 minutes or just until set on the outer edges. Remove from the pan of water and cool to room temperature. Chill in the refrigerator.

Combine the mango with lime juice and sugar to taste in the blender container and process until smooth.

Loosen the edge of the custards with a knife and invert onto serving plates. Serve with mango sauce. Garnish with raspberries and confectioners' sugar.

NOTEWORTHY NIGHTS
INFORMAL DINNERS

the menus

Sonata for Six
Springtime Airs
Mediterranean Melody
Casual Concerto
Divertimento

the music

Mendelssohn: Symphony No. 4
Music from *A Midsummer Night's Dream*
Telarc CD-80318

Barber: Violin Concerto/Souvenirs/Piano Concerto
Telarc CD-80441

"Classical Zoo"
Telarc CD-80443

SONATA FOR SIX

no cause for alarm

In his *1812 Overture*, Tchaikovsky calls for the firing of military cannons, but orchestras often simulate them by setting off explosive charges. At a 1974 Atlanta Symphony Orchestra concert, smoke from the explosives set off the fire alarm backstage. When the audience emerged after the concert, they found fire engines and firemen with hoses at the ready. After *Time* magazine got wind of the story, Robert Shaw commented, "As the smoke cleared and firemen in full asbestos regalia appeared marching down the aisles, it became apparent that what I had mistaken in the din of battle as a premature entry of the chimes had been an over-eager automated smell-all and tell-all that didn't know its brass from principal bass."

Nick Jones, Atlanta Symphony Orchestra
Program Annotator and Chorus Member

GRILLED *eggplant* ON WILTED *greens*

spicy california merlot

BRAISED *lamb shanks*

risotto MILANESE

STEAMED GREEN *peas* WITH MINT

australian shiraz

pear pie WITH VANILLA ICE CREAM

flavored coffee

Grilled Eggplant on Wilted Greens   serves six

eggplant

2   (8-ounce) Japanese eggplant
1   tablespoon olive oil
1/2 teaspoon salt
1/2 teaspoon pepper

salad

3   cups mixed field greens
1   small red onion, thinly sliced
•   fresh lemon juice to taste
2   tablespoons extra-virgin olive oil
1   tablespoon reduced-sodium
     soy sauce
1   tablespoon seasoned rice vinegar

Serve this first course with crostini recipe on page 95, dusted with fresh parsley.

For the eggplant, cut off and discard the ends of the eggplant. Peel the eggplant or leave the peel intact as preferred. Slice lengthwise into about 8 slices, 1/2 inch thick.

Rub both sides with the olive oil and sprinkle with the salt and pepper. Let stand for 10 minutes. Grill the eggplant slices over very hot coals or cook in a heated nonstick skillet for 3 minutes on each side.

For the salad, mound the field greens on serving plates. Top with the eggplant slices, cutting pieces of larger eggplant into bite sizes if preferred. Arrange the onion slices over the top and drizzle with lemon juice.

Whisk the olive oil, soy sauce and vinegar in a small bowl until smooth. Drizzle over the salad and serve immediately.

Braised Lamb Shanks

serves six

ingredients

6	medium lamb shanks, about 6 pounds
•	salt and pepper to taste
3	tablespoons olive oil
10	carrots, peeled, chopped
12	garlic cloves, minced
2	large purple onions, chopped
2	teaspoons dried rosemary
2	teaspoons dried oregano
2	(28-ounce) cans diced tomatoes
3	cups dry red wine
2	tablespoons grated lemon zest
1	teaspoon salt
2	teaspoons crushed red pepper
1	teaspoon black pepper

This dish is easier to prepare if you ask the butcher to cut the shanks into halves crosswise.

Sprinkle the lamb with salt and pepper to taste. Brown in a single layer in the heated olive oil in a heavy saucepan over medium-high heat for 10 minutes per shank. Remove the shanks to a bowl as they brown.

Add the carrots, garlic and onions to the drippings in the saucepan. Cook over medium heat until tender. Add the rosemary, oregano, undrained tomatoes, wine and lemon zest. Stir in the salt, red pepper and black pepper.

Return the lamb and any accumulated juices to the saucepan. Cook over very low heat for 2 hours or until the lamb is tender enough to fall from the bone. Remove the lamb to a bowl.

Cook the sauce until reduced to the desired consistency. Add the lamb and cook just until heated through. Serve the lamb over Risotto Milanese (page 86); spoon the sauce over the top.

Braised Lamb Shanks / Risotto Milanese on page 86

Risotto Milanese

ingredients

5 cups chicken broth
3 tablespoons butter
2 tablespoons olive oil
1 1/2 small yellow onions, chopped
1 (12-ounce) package arborio rice
1 1/2 cups dry white wine
• large pinch of saffron threads
• salt and freshly ground pepper
    to taste
1/2 cup grated Parmesan cheese

Heat the chicken broth to just below the simmering point in a medium saucepan; keep hot.

Melt the butter with the olive oil in a large heavy saucepan. Add the onions and sauté for 10 minutes or until golden brown. Add the rice and cook for 5 minutes, stirring constantly with a wooden spoon to coat well. Add the wine and cook for several minutes or until the wine is absorbed, stirring constantly.

Add the hot broth to the rice 1/2 cup at a time, cooking until the liquid is absorbed after each addition and stirring frequently; the rice should be tender after about 20 minutes.

Stir in the saffron, salt and pepper. Remove the saucepan from the heat and stir in the Parmesan cheese. Serve immediately.

Steamed Green Peas with Mint

serves six

ingredients

1 pound fresh peas
1 tablespoon melted butter
• salt to taste
2 tablespoons hot water
1 teaspoon chopped fresh mint,
    thyme or other fresh herb

Combine the peas with the melted butter and salt in a saucepan, shaking to coat well. Add the hot water. Cook, covered, for 10 minutes or until the peas are tender. Add the mint just before serving.

Pear Pie

cheese pastry

I	cup flour
1/4	teaspoon salt
1/3	cup shortening
1/2	cup shredded Cheddar cheese
3	or 4 tablespoons ice water

pear filling

5 1/2	cups sliced peeled pears, about 3 pounds
2	teaspoons lemon juice
1/2	cup sugar
1/4	cup flour
1/4	teaspoon cinnamon

crumb topping

3/4	cup packed light brown sugar
1/2	cup flour
1/3	cup butter or margarine

For the pastry, mix the flour and salt in a medium bowl. Cut in the shortening until the mixture resembles coarse crumbs. Mix in the cheese. Sprinkle with the ice water I tablespoon at a time, tossing with a fork after each addition until the mixture is moist enough to hold together.

Shape into a ball and flatten slightly on a lightly floured surface. Roll to fit into a 10- or 11-inch pie plate; trim and crimp the edge.

For the filling, toss the pears with the lemon juice in a large bowl. Mix the sugar, flour and cinnamon together and add to the pears; toss to mix well. Spoon into the pie shell.

For the topping, mix the brown sugar and flour in a bowl. Cut in the butter until the mixture resemble coarse crumbs. Sprinkle over the pears.

Bake the pie at 375 degrees for I hour. Cool on a wire rack.

Note: *Do not use low-calorie margarine for the topping of this pie, as it will not bind the flour and brown sugar.*

SPRINGTIME AIRS

and they all came

During the Atlanta Symphony Orchestra's 50th Anniversary in 1994–1995, the orchestra and the Symphony Associates presented Symphony Celebration/A Musical Open House and invited all of Atlanta. So many came that Orchestra President Allison Vulgamore had to step back quickly as the doors opened and the crowd flowed onto the musical streets. Record numbers arrived throughout the day and packed Symphony Hall that evening for the Robert Shaw Sing-along. Atlantans of all ages sent thank-you notes for weeks. Symphony Celebration later received an American Symphony Orchestra League Sally Parker Education Award.

Carla Fackler
Atlanta Symphony Associates President
   1994–1996

CHILLED *cauliflower soup*

salmon fillet WITH *couscous*
AND *orange mustard* SAUCE

STEAMED SUGAR *snap peas*

california fumé blanc

WHITE CHOCOLATE *cheesecake*

Chilled Cauliflower Soup

serves four

ingredients

2   large onions, chopped
5   tablespoons butter
2   pounds fresh or frozen
      cauliflower, chopped
$1/4$ cup flour
1   teaspoon curry powder
2   cups (or more) chicken stock
2   cups whole milk
3   bay leaves
$1/2$ to 1 cup cream (optional)
•   sherry to taste (optional)
•   salt and pepper to taste

garnish

•   paprika or chopped parsley

Sauté the onions in the melted butter in a large saucepan over low heat until tender. Add the cauliflower and cook for several minutes, stirring occasionally.

Sprinkle with the flour and curry powder. Cook for 2 minutes, stirring frequently. Stir in the chicken stock and milk. Add the bay leaves. Cook until thickened, stirring constantly. Cook, covered, for 45 minutes, adding additional chicken stock if needed for the desired consistency.

Transfer the mixture to a blender container, discarding the bay leaves. Process until smooth. Combine with the cream and sherry in a bowl and mix well. Season with salt and pepper to taste.

Chill until serving time. Ladle into soup bowls and garnish with paprika or parsley.

Note: *This soup can also be served hot.*

Salmon Fillet with Couscous and Orange Mustard Sauce

serves four

ingredients

I	tablespoon peanut oil
I	recipe Couscous (page 91)
4	(6-ounce) salmon fillets
•	salt and pepper to taste
5	tablespoons peanut oil
I	recipe Orange Mustard Sauce (page 91)
I	red bell pepper, cut into small diamond shapes
I	green bell pepper, cut into small diamond shapes
I	yellow bell pepper, cut into small diamond shapes
1/2	cup chick-peas
2	teaspoons chopped chives

Heat a small sauté pan over medium heat and add I tablespoon peanut oil. Add the Couscous and cook for 2 minutes, stirring constantly. Spoon the mixture into the centers of 4 warmed plates.

Cut the salmon fillets into halves lengthwise and season with salt and pepper. Heat 5 tablespoons peanut oil in the same sauté pan and add the salmon. Sauté until the salmon flakes easily, turning once. Arrange over the couscous.

Wipe the sauté pan with a paper towel and add the Orange Mustard Sauce, bell peppers and chick-peas. Cook for 3 minutes. Season with salt and pepper. Spoon around the fillets and couscous and sprinkle with the chives. Serve immediately.

Couscous

ingredients

16   ounces uncooked couscous
2   cups chicken stock
1   teaspoon salt
1/2 teaspoon freshly ground
     white pepper
4   teaspoons chopped dried dates
1   teaspoon grated orange zest
1   teaspoon chopped fresh
     mint leaves
1   teaspoon chopped fresh
     cilantro leaves
1   teaspoon orange-flower water
•   Tabasco sauce to taste
1/2 teaspoon cinnamon

Heat a medium saucepan over medium heat. Add the couscous, chicken stock, salt and white pepper. Cook for 10 to 15 minutes or until tender, stirring constantly.

Add the dates, orange zest, mint, cilantro, orange-flower water, Tabasco sauce and cinnamon and mix well. Correct the seasoning and cook until heated through.

Orange Mustard Sauce

ingredients

1   teaspoon ginger liqueur
1   teaspoon chopped shallot
1   cup orange juice
1/2 teaspoon chopped candied ginger
1/2 cup Dijon mustard
1   tablespoon orange marmelade
1   cup heavy cream
1/2 teaspoon salt
1/4 teaspoon freshly ground
     white pepper

Heat a medium saucepan over medium heat. Add the ginger liqueur and shallot. Cook until the liqueur evaporates. Stir in the orange juice and candied ginger. Cook until the liquid nearly evaporates.

Stir in the Dijon mustard, orange marmelade, cream, salt and white pepper. Cook until reduced to a syrupy consistency, stirring frequently. Correct the seasoning.

White Chocolate Cheesecake   serves twelve

ingredients

2¹/4 cups crushed gingersnaps, about
        16 cookies (page 93)
3   tablespoons melted butter
40   ounces cream cheese, softened
1³/4 cups sugar
¹/4   cup flour
1   tablespoon vanilla extract
8   ounces white chocolate, melted
5   eggs
2   egg yolks
¹/4   cup half-and-half

Use the recipe on page 93 for homemade gingersnaps or, if time is limited, substitute commercial gingersnaps.

Mix the cookie crumbs and butter in a bowl. Press over bottom and side of a buttered 9- or 10-inch springform pan. Chill in the refrigerator.

Beat the cream cheese at low speed in a mixing bowl until light. Add the sugar, flour, vanilla and white chocolate and beat until smooth. Beat in the eggs and egg yolks 1 at a time. Add the half-and-half and mix until smooth. Pour into the prepared crust.

Bake at 400 degrees for 10 minutes. Reduce the oven temperature to 200 degrees. Bake for 1¹/2 hours longer or until the center is nearly set.

Turn off the oven. Let the cheesecake stand in the closed oven for 1¹/2 hours longer or until it is firm and cool. Chill for 8 hours or longer before serving.

Note: *You may reserve and color ¹/4 cup of the filling for seasonal decorations for the top of the cheesecake.*

Gingersnaps

ingredients

2	cups flour
1	tablespoon baking powder
1	teaspoon ground cloves
1	teaspoon ground cinnamon
1	teaspoon ground ginger
1/4	teaspoon salt
3/4	cup butter, softened
1	cup sugar
1/4	cup light molasses
1	egg, lightly beaten
1/3	cup sugar

Sift the flour, baking powder, cloves, cinnamon, ginger and salt together. Cream the butter with 1 cup sugar in a mixing bowl until light and fluffy. Beat in the molasses and egg. Add the sifted ingredients and mix just until smooth.

Chill, covered, for 1 hour or longer. Shape into 1-inch balls and roll in 1/3 cup sugar. Arrange 2 inches apart on ungreased cookie sheets.

Bake at 350 degrees for 10 to 12 minutes or until brown on the bottom. Let stand on the cookie sheets for 1 minute, then remove to a wire rack to cool completely. Store at room temperature in an airtight container.

MEDITERRANEAN MELODY

a chilling experience

I traveled with my husband, a former Atlanta Symphony Orchestra musician, on the European tour led by Yoel Levi in 1991. One morning while I took my bath, Warren put the suitcases in the hall for pick-up and went down to eat breakfast. To my surprise, he had packed the clothes I put out to wear that day! I ended up flying from Vienna to Zurich in my little blue nightie and my purple raincoat!

Jane Little, Assistant Principal Bass
[Jane Little has played with the Atlanta Symphony Orchestra since its first concert in 1945!]

MESCLUN WITH *roasted tomato* VINAIGRETTE

CROSTINI WITH WILD *mushroom ragout*

crisp pinot grigio

cioppino PAISANO

italian chianti classico

tortoni WITH CHOCOLATE GANACHE

CRANBERRY *biscotti*

Crostini with Wild Mushroom Ragout   serves six

crostini

1/2   loaf French bread
2   tablespoons olive oil
2   garlic cloves, cut into halves

mushroom ragout

5   ounces domestic or wild
      mushrooms, or a combination
1   tablespoon unsalted butter
2   teaspoons peanut oil or olive oil
1   small onion, chopped
3   garlic cloves
1   tablespoon chopped fresh parsley
1   tablespoon chopped fresh thyme
•   salt and pepper to taste
1/2   cup dry white wine

For the crostini, cut the bread into thin slices and arrange on a baking sheet. Drizzle with the olive oil. Rub the cut sides of the garlic over both sides of the bread.

Bake at 350 degrees until golden brown and just crisp. Cool to room temperature.

For the ragout, chop the mushrooms into 2-inch pieces. Heat the butter and peanut oil in a large skillet over medium heat. Add the onion and sauté for several minutes. Add the mushrooms and increase the heat to medium-high. Sauté for 3 minutes or until the mushrooms yield their liquid.

Stir in the garlic, parsley, thyme, salt and pepper. Add the wine and cook for 5 minutes or until the liquid is reduced and thickened. Spoon onto the crostini to serve.

Note: *The ragout can be made several days in advance and stored in the refrigerator. Simmer for 5 minutes to reheat.*

Crostini with Wild Mushroom Ragout on page 95 / Mesclun with Roasted Tomato Vinaigrette

Roasted Tomato Vinaigrette

serves six

ingredients

2   teaspoons red wine vinegar
2   teaspoons balsamic vinegar
3   tablespoons extra-virgin olive oil
1   small yellow onion, chopped
1   tablespoon finely chopped
     fresh basil
1   recipe Oven-Roasted Tomatoes
     (page 52), cooled, coarsely
     chopped
1/2 teaspoon salt
•   freshly ground pepper

Combine the wine vinegar and balsamic vinegar in a bowl. Add the olive oil gradually, mixing until smooth. Stir in the onion, basil and Oven-Roasted Tomatoes. Season with salt and pepper to taste.

Chill until serving time. Serve over a salad of mesclun.

Note: *For the best vinaigrette, choose a balsamic vinegar labeled* Tradizionale, *made from 100% cooked aged white grapes. Use cold-pressed extra-virgin olive oil for the most delicious results.*

Cioppino Paisano

ingredients

1¹/₂ cups chopped onions
3   garlic cloves, minced
2   teaspoons olive oil
1¹/₂ cups dry white wine
2   (14-ounce) cans chicken broth
1   (28-ounce) can stewed tomatoes
¹/₂ teaspoon hot sauce
1   teaspoon dried basil
1   teaspoon dried thyme
¹/₄ teaspoon saffron
¹/₄ teaspoon salt
16   mussels
3   to 4 pounds medium shrimp,
     peeled
4   pounds sea bass or cod, cut into
     1-inch pieces

Sauté the onions and garlic in the heated olive oil in a large saucepan for 5 minutes or until tender. Add the wine, chicken broth, undrained tomatoes, hot sauce, basil, thyme, saffron and salt. Bring to a boil and reduce the heat. Simmer for 30 minutes, stirring occasionally.

Cook the mussels in water to cover in a saucepan until the shells open. Add the mussels to the broth mixture, adding enough of the mussel cooking liquid to make of the desired consistency. Add the shrimp and fish. Cook until the shrimp are opaque and the fish flakes easily.

Cranberry Biscotti

makes two and one-half dozen

ingredients

2¹/4 cups flour
1 cup sugar
1 teaspoon baking powder
¹/2 teaspoon baking soda
1 teaspoon cinnamon
1 teaspoon nutmeg
2 eggs
2 egg whites
1 tablespoon almond extract
1 tablespoon vanilla extract
1¹/4 cups sweetened dried cranberries
³/4 cup whole almonds

Mix the flour, sugar, baking powder, baking soda, cinnamon and nutmeg in a large mixing bowl. Whisk the eggs, egg whites and flavorings together in a medium bowl. Add to the dry ingredients and mix at medium speed just until moistened. Stir in the cranberries and almonds; mix well.

Divide the dough into 2 portions on a floured surface. Shape each portion into a log 14 inches long and 1¹/2 inches in diameter. Place on a cookie sheet.

Bake at 325 degrees for 30 minutes. Remove from the oven and reduce the oven temperature to 300 degrees.

Cut the logs into ¹/2-inch slices with a sharp or serrated knife. Stand slices upright on the cookie sheet. Bake for 15 minutes longer. Cool on a wire rack. Store in a loosely covered container.

Tortoni with Chocolate Ganache serves six

ingredients

1	teaspoon unflavored gelatin
1	tablespoon cold water
1	cup sugar
1/2	cup water
1/4	teaspoon salt
6	egg yolks, beaten
3/4	cup crushed macaroons
1/2	cup chopped walnuts
1/2	cup chopped blanched almonds
1	teaspoon vanilla extract
2	cups whipping cream, whipped
1	recipe Chocolate Ganache (page 65)
1/4	cup chopped blanched almonds

Soften the gelatin in 1 tablespoon cold water in a bowl for 5 minutes.

Combine the sugar, 1/2 cup water and salt in a saucepan and bring to a boil. Cook to 230 degrees on a candy thermometer, spun-thread stage. Add the mixture very gradually to the egg yolks, stirring constantly.

Add the softened gelatin and mix until the gelatin dissolves completely. Let stand until cool. Fold in the crushed macaroons, walnuts, 1/2 cup almonds and vanilla. Fold in the whipped cream. Spoon into 6 molds. Freeze until firm.

Drizzle each plate with the Chocolate Ganache. Dip each mold into hot water and invert immediately onto the prepared plates. Sprinkle with 1/4 cup almonds.

Note: *This can also be prepared in 12 smaller molds to serve more people.*

Tortoni with Chocolate Ganache

CASUAL CONCERTO

don't their feet look great?

Someone generously gave every gentleman in the orchestra a pair of shiny, new patent leather shoes. They looked good but weren't very expensive. Everyone wore them except Bill [William Preucil, Concertmaster at the time], who had expensive leather shoes. We were on tour in Missouri, and someone I knew there said, "You know, everybody looks great. The men's shoes are so nice and shiny, except for the Concertmaster. Can't he afford a nice pair of new shoes?"

Mark Yancich, Principal Timpani

lima bean SPREAD
PITA TRIANGLES WITH BABY CHERRY TOMATOES

mixed greens WITH BALSAMIC VINEGAR,
OLIVE OIL, LEMON WEDGES, PARMESAN CHEESE,
AND FRESHLY GROUND PEPPER

ROAST *chicken* WITH *fennel* AND *artichokes*

FRENCH *baguette*

slightly chilled pinot noir

hazelnut BROWNIES

Lima Bean Spread

serves four

ingredients

1   (10-ounce) package frozen
     lima beans
4   garlic cloves, crushed
1   teaspoon salt
1/4 teaspoon crushed red pepper
1 1/2 tablespoons extra-virgin olive oil
•   juice of 2 lemons
1   teaspoon ground cumin
•   salt and freshly ground black
     pepper to taste
3   tablespoons chopped fresh mint

Bring a large saucepan of water to a boil. Add the lima beans, garlic, 1 teaspoon salt and crushed red pepper. Cook for 10 minutes or until the beans are tender. Let the beans cool in the cooking liquid.

Drain the beans and place in the food processor container. Add the olive oil, lemon juice and cumin and process until smooth. Season with salt and black pepper to taste.

Spoon into a bowl and stir in the mint. Store, covered, in the refrigerator for up to 4 days or in the freezer for up to 6 months.

Serve with warmed pita triangles and sweet cherry tomatoes.

Roast Chicken with Fennel and Artichokes

serves four

ingredients

8	large shallots
6	ripe tomatoes, cut into quarters
1	(9-ounce) package frozen artichoke hearts, thawed
1	fresh fennel bulb, trimmed, cut lengthwise into eighths
1	garlic bulb, cloves separated but unpeeled
2/3	cup Niçoise or other brine-cured olives
1/4	cup fresh lemon juice
2	tablespoons chopped fresh thyme, or 2 teaspoons dried thyme
•	salt and pepper to taste
1	cup canned chicken broth
1	(4-pound) roasting chicken, butterflied with bones in

Combine the shallots, tomatoes, artichoke hearts, fennel, garlic and olives in a large roasting pan. Pour the lemon juice evenly over the vegetables. Sprinkle with the thyme, salt and pepper.

Pour the chicken broth into the pan and cover with foil. Roast at 350 degrees on the center oven rack for 20 minutes.

Increase the oven temperature to 450 degrees. Place the chicken on the vegetables. Roast for 20 minutes or until the chicken is tender and brown, basting frequently.

Remove the chicken to a serving platter. Remove the vegetables with a slotted spoon, reserving the garlic and cooking liquid. Arrange the vegetables around the chicken.

Press the garlic cloves from the skins and combine with the cooking liquid in a food processor container. Process until smooth, adding additional chicken broth if needed for the desired consistency. Serve with the chicken and vegetables.

Hazelnut Brownies

hazelnut filling

4	ounces cream cheese, softened
1/4	cup sugar
1	large egg
2	teaspoons lemon juice
2	teaspoons vanilla extract
1/4	cup finely ground toasted hazelnuts or almonds

brownies

2	cups semisweet chocolate chips
2	tablespoons plus 2 teaspoons butter
1 1/2	cups flour
1/4	cup baking cocoa
1	teaspoon baking powder
1/2	teaspoon salt
1 1/2	cups sugar
4	large eggs
2	teaspoons vanilla extract
1	cup coarsely chopped toasted hazelnuts or almonds

For the filling, beat the cream cheese with the sugar at medium speed in a mixing bowl until smooth. Beat in the egg, lemon juice and vanilla. Fold in the hazelnuts. Set aside.

For the brownies, melt the chocolate chips with the butter in a double boiler over low heat, whisking to mix well. Cool to room temperature. Sift the flour, baking cocoa, baking powder and salt together.

Combine the sugar, eggs and vanilla in a mixing bowl and beat for 2 minutes or until pale yellow and smooth. Beat in the melted chocolate. Add the flour mixture and mix well. Fold in the hazelnuts.

Spread half the chocolate batter in a greased 8x10-inch baking pan. Spread the filling over the chocolate and top with the remaining chocolate batter. Swirl with a knife to marbleize.

Bake at 350 degrees for 50 minutes. Cool on a wire rack and cut into squares.

Note: *The filling can be prepared 1 day in advance and stored, covered, in the refrigerator until needed.*

for six

DIVERTIMENTO

while you're at it

In the late 1980s, I invited several Atlanta Symphony Orchestra staff members to a picnic outside the Arts Center. As I was dragging the heavy picnic table and chairs into the sun, the stage doors flew open and half a dozen people poured out, including Yoel Levi and the Telarc recording manager. I quickly discovered that my dragging efforts had disrupted the orchestra's recording session! Apologizing profusely, I asked if there was anything I could do to make it up to them. Motioning to a large backhoe tearing up the street, Yoel jokingly asked, "While you're at it, can you stop them too?" Still mortified, I marched over, and, after making several choice comments about how much it would cost per hour, they did indeed stop!

Marcy McTier
Atlanta Symphony Associates President
1990–1992

gulf crab fritter WITH AVOCADO AND CITRUS

napa valley trefethen dry riesling

SAUTÉED *turbot* WITH BABY *spinach,*
SPROUTED *beans* AND SOY BUTTER

north coast signorello pinot noir

PEAR, *endive, stilton* AND WALNUT *salad* WITH
pear VINAIGRETTE

WARM VALRHONA *chocolate cake* WITH
VANILLA BEAN ICE CREAM

california quadyessensia orange muscat

FROM *Bacchanalia*

Gulf Crab Fritter with Avocado and Citrus

mayonnaise

1	egg
1	egg yolk
•	juice of 1 lemon
1/2	tablespoon Dijon mustard
1 1/2	cups canola oil or peanut oil
•	salt and freshly ground white pepper to taste

fritters

8	ounces shredded blue crab meat, steamed
•	Tabasco sauce and salt to taste
•	panko (Japanese bread crumbs) for coating
•	peanut oil for frying

accompaniments

1	orange
1	blood orange
1	grapefruit
1	pink grapefruit
1	lime
1	tangerine
2	firm ripe avocados, sliced
•	Thai Pepper Essence (page 108)
•	Vanilla Oil (page 108)

garnish

•	coriander and chives

For the mayonnaise, combine the egg, egg yolk, lemon juice and Dijon mustard in a food processor and process until smooth. Drizzle in the canola oil, processing constantly until the desired consistency is reached. Season with salt and white pepper to taste.

For the fritters, combine the crab meat with 1/4 cup of the mayonnaise, Tabasco sauce and salt to taste in a bowl and mix well. Shape into six balls and coat well with the bread crumbs.

Heat 1 inch of peanut oil to 350 degrees in a saucepan or skillet. Add the fritters and fry until golden brown.

To serve, section the orange, blood orange, grapefruit, pink grapefruit, lime and tangerine. Serve the fritters with the avocados, citrus sections, Thai Pepper Essence and Vanilla Oil. Garnish with coriander and chives.

Note: *Panko can be found in well-stocked supermarkets and Asian markets.*

Thai Pepper Essence

makes one cup

ingredients

3   fresh Thai peppers
1   fresh red chile pepper
2   garlic cloves, chopped
•   juice of 3 limes
2   tablespoons nam pla (Thai fish sauce)
$^1/_2$ cup maple syrup

Chop the Thai peppers and chile pepper, discarding the seeds. Combine the peppers and garlic in a bowl. Add the lime juice, nam pla and maple syrup and mix well. Chill for 1 hour or longer.

Note: *Nam pla can be found in well-stocked supermarkets and Asian markets.*

Vanilla Oil

makes one cup

ingredients

1   vanilla bean
1   cup grapeseed oil or canola oil

Split the vanilla bean and scrape the seeds into a glass jar. Add the bean and the grapeseed oil to the jar and mix well. Let stand for 1 hour.

Sautéed Turbot with Baby Spinach, Sprouted Beans and Soy Butter serves six

soy butter

1   shallot, chopped
1/2   cup white wine
1/2   cup heavy cream
1/2   cup butter, chilled, chopped
1/4   cup soy sauce
•   juice of 1 lemon

turbot

6   (6-ounce) turbot or snapper fillets
1   (8-ounce) package panko
      (Japanese bread crumbs)
1   tablespoon olive oil
2   pounds baby spinach
6   ounces sprouted soy beans, or
      other sprouted beans
1   tablespoon olive oil
•   sea salt to taste
•   lemon juice to taste

For the soy butter, combine the shallot and wine in a heavy saucepan. Cook over medium heat until almost the liquid is gone. Add the cream. Cook until almost all the liquid is gone. Remove from the heat and whisk in the butter. Add the soy sauce and lemon juice; keep warm.

For the turbot, coat the fillets with panko. Heat 1 tablespoon olive oil in a nonstick skillet. Add the turbot and cook for 1 minute on each side or until golden brown.

Sauté the spinach and sprouted beans in 1 tablespoon olive oil just until wilted. Spoon the mixture into the centers of six serving plates. Sprinkle with sea salt and drizzle with lemon juice.

Drizzle the soy butter around the edge of the plate and top the spinach with the fillets. Serve immediately.

Note: *Panko can be found in well-stocked supermarkets and Asian markets.*

Pear, Endive, Stilton and Walnut Salad with Pear Vinaigrette

serves six

pear vinaigrette

2   soft ripe red Comice pears
1   cup white vinegar
1/4   cup clover honey
1   cup walnut oil
1   teaspoon salt
1/4   teaspoon freshly ground white pepper

salad

3   firm red Comice pears
6   whole Belgian endives
1/3   cup toasted walnut pieces
6   ounces English Stilton cheese or bleu cheese

garnish

•   cut champagne grapes or seedless red grapes

For the vinaigrette, peel, core and coarsely chop the pears. Combine with the vinegar in a heavy saucepan. Cook over medium heat until the liquid is reduced by 1/2. Process in the food processor until smooth. Add the honey and process until smooth. Add the walnut oil gradually, processing constantly until smooth. Season with salt and white pepper. Store in an airtight container in the refrigerator for up to 1 week. Stir to mix before using.

For the salad, cut the pears into thin slices. Cut the endives crosswise into thin slices. Combine the pears and endives in a bowl and add the desired amount of vinaigrette; toss to coat well. Arrange on the serving plates and top with the walnuts and cheese. Garnish with grapes.

Warm Valrhona Chocolate Cake with Vanilla Bean Ice Cream

serves six

ingredients

3/4 cup butter
6 ounces Valrhona or extra-bitter chocolate
3 eggs
3 egg yolks
5 3/4 tablespoons sugar
7 tablespoons flour

garnish

• mint sprigs

Melt the butter and chocolate slowly in a double boiler, stirring to mix and melt completely. Beat the whole eggs, egg yolks and sugar at medium speed in a mixing bowl for 10 minutes or until pale yellow, thickened and increased four times in volume. Add the flour gradually, beating at low speed. Stir in the chocolate gradually by hand with a rubber spatula.

Pour into six lightly buttered and floured individual pans; do not use bundt pans. Bake at 320 degrees in a convection oven for 7 to 8 minutes. Bake at 350 degrees in a conventional oven for 10 to 12 minutes or until the center still looks soft and the outside rim of top is firm. Invert the cakes on plates and serve immediately with vanilla bean ice cream and a garnish of mint.

GREAT MASTERPIECES
FORMAL DINNERS

the menus

Elegant Impressions
Savory Symphony
Major Composition
Rhapsody in Dining

the music

Haydn: The Creation
Telarc CD-80298

Sibelius: Symphonies No. 1 and No. 5
Telarc CD-80246

"Absolute Heaven"
Telarc CD-80458

Mahler: Symphony No. 4/Songs of a Wayfarer
Telarc CD-80499

ELEGANT IMPRESSIONS

mahler at carnegie

The Atlanta Symphony Orchestra
Chorus sang the Mahler 8th Symphony
in a 1996 Carnegie Hall concert
featuring several choruses. Hundreds of
singers joined the orchestra on stage or
performed from the first two rows of
boxes circling the hall. The audience
was basically surrounded. Following
the crashing ending, the audience was
so overwhelmed, they didn't know where
to look to applaud. They were looking
in the back, at the stage, this way, that
way, everywhere. The sound was just
all-enveloping.

Sam Marley, Symphony Chorus Member

watercress SOUP

ravioli TERRINE

french chablis

sea bass BAKED IN PARCHMENT

SAUTÉED *brussels sprout* LEAVES

brut champagne

LEMON *sorbet* WITH CASSIS
CHOCOLATE *truffles*

Watercress Soup

ingredients

I	tablespoon canola oil or olive oil
•	leaves and stems of I medium bunch watercress
I	rib celery with leaves, chopped
I	large yellow onion, coarsely chopped
3	garlic cloves
3	cups unsalted chicken stock
I	medium baking potato, peeled, cut into 2-inch cubes
3/4	teaspoon salt

garnish

•	croutons
•	watercress leaves

Heat the canola oil in a saucepan. Add the watercress, celery, onion and garlic. Sauté over medium heat for 5 minutes. Add the chicken stock, potatoes and salt. Bring to a boil and reduce the heat to low. Simmer, covered, for 30 minutes.

Process the mixture in a food processor until puréed. Return to the saucepan and heat over low heat just until heated through; do not boil.

Ladle into soup bowls. Garnish with 2 or 3 small croutons and watercress leaves.

Note: *The soup may be made in advance and stored in the refrigerator; cover the surface directly with plastic wrap. Reheat over low heat to serve.*

Ravioli Terrine

Ravioli Terrine

ingredients

2   large packages frozen round or
    square cheese ravioli
2   to 4 large leeks
2   teaspoons salt
8   large oven-roasted plum tomatoes
    (page 52)
8   large scallions, chopped
1   large red bell pepper,
    finely chopped
6   small anchovy fillets, minced
2/3 cup finely chopped
    kalamata olives
1   teaspoon chile paste, or
    Tabasco to taste
1   (3 1/2-ounce) jar capers, drained,
    chopped
1/4 cup chopped fresh basil
    or oregano
2   tablespoons olive oil
2   small bulbs garlic, roasted, minced
•   salt and pepper to taste
1 1/2 cups raspberry vinaigrette

Line a loaf pan or collapsible terrine pan with plastic wrap, allowing enough to cover the terrine. Cook the ravioli using the package directions.

Clean the leeks by running cold water through the stalk. Trim the bottom and wash again. Bring a large shallow pan of water to a boil and add 2 teaspoons salt. Add the leeks and poach for 3 minutes or until the tops wilt slightly. Remove to a cold water bath and cool; drain.

Peel the green leaves from the leeks and lay flat on a work surface. Line the loaf pan completely with the leaves, arranging to drape over the edges of the pan and leaving enough to cover the terrine; arrange in lattice or other creative design if desired.

Combine the tomatoes, scallions, bell pepper, anchovies, olives, chile paste, capers and basil in a small bowl. Drizzle with the olive oil and toss to coat well. Add the garlic and season with salt and pepper to taste.

Arrange a layer of ravioli in the prepared loaf pan. Layer the tomato mixture and remaining ravioli 1/3 at a time in the pan, completely covering the top with ravioli; there may be leftover ravioli.

Fold the leek leaves over the top and press down lightly. Fold the plastic wrap over the leeks. Wrap again with plastic wrap and top with a heavy object to compact the terrine. Chill in the refrigerator for 8 hours or longer.

Lift the terrine gently from the pan using the plastic wrap. Open the plastic wrap, place a serving plate over the top and invert onto the dish; discard the plastic wrap. Slice with a serrated knife to serve. Drizzle servings with raspberry vinaigrette.

Sea Bass Baked in Parchment

serves four

ingredients

2   tablespoons olive oil

$1/4$ cup lemon juice

9   small cherry tomatoes,
       cut into halves

4   small artichoke hearts, chopped

$1/4$ cup chopped green onions
       with tops

4   hearts of palm, sliced

3   tablespoons chopped basil leaves

•   salt and pepper to taste

4   (8- or 9-ounce) sea bass fillets

•   green onion stems

garnish

•   caviar

Combine the olive oil, lemon juice, tomatoes, artichoke hearts, $1/4$ cup green onions, hearts of palm, basil, salt and pepper in a large shallow dish. Add the fish. Marinate in the refrigerator for 1 hour or longer.

Prepare 4 large squares of parchment. Place 1 fish fillet on each square and spoon the marinade over the top, dividing the vegetables evenly. Wrap the fish in the parchment as for a present and tie with green onion stems.

Arrange the bundles in a baking pan. Place in a 450-degree oven on the middle or top oven rack to prevent the parchment from burning. Bake for 15 minutes. Serve from the parchment or remove to serving plates. Garnish servings with caviar.

Note: *The fish has a buttery flavor; white wine can be substituted for the olive oil.*

Sea Bass Baked in Parchment

for eight
SAVORY SYMPHONY

taking the shirt off his back

When I played in the Atlantic Symphony, we were on tour and had just arrived for the last concert in the dead of winter. We were warming up backstage when our stage manager approached me and announced in a loud voice that Victor Yampoiski, our music director, wanted to see me in his dressing room. Everyone stared as I walked out and quickly returned without my tuxedo shirt. Victor had forgotten his at the hotel and the staff guessed that we were the same size. Wearing my only other option, something bright blue and casual, I played on, knowing that Victor owed me one during the next rehearsal series!

Joe Riedel
Atlanta Symphony Orchestra Board Member
[CEO of Beers Construction Company, Joe Riedel was formerly a professional trombonist who played in the Atlantic Symphony of Halifax, Nova Scotia.]

ROASTED *onion* AND *garlic* SOUP

SPICY *parmesan crackers*

MIXED GREENS WITH *oranges* AND *honey~soy* DRESSING

spanish rioja

PESTO *pork* WITH *gingered plum* SAUCE

STEAMED *bok choy*

côtes du rhone red

pears IN RED WINE

flavored coffees

cordials

Roasted Onion and Garlic Soup   serves eight

ingredients

1	garlic bulb
1	tablespoon olive oil
4	medium yellow onions
3	tablespoons olive oil
2	quarts canned chicken broth
•	salt and pepper to taste
2	potatoes, peeled, chopped, about 2 cups

garnish

3	tablespoons chopped fresh thyme or parsley

This soup has a wonderful garlic flavor. Serve just enough to whet the appetite before the meal.

Cut off the top of the entire unpeeled garlic bulb. Drizzle 1 tablespoon olive oil into the individual cloves. Rub the unpeeled whole onions with 2 tablespoons of the remaining olive oil. Place the onions in a roasting pan. Roast at 350 degrees for 30 minutes. Add the garlic bulb to the pan. Roast for 30 minutes longer or until the vegetables are tender when pricked with the tip of a sharp knife. Let stand until cool enough to handle; peel. Mash the garlic and chop the onions.

Heat the remaining 1 tablespoon olive oil in a large saucepan. Sauté onions in the heated olive oil for 15 minutes. Add the garlic, chicken broth, salt and pepper. Bring to a boil and reduce the heat. Simmer for 20 minutes. Add the potatoes and simmer for 30 minutes longer or until tender.

Cool the soup to room temperature. Process in batches in the food processor until puréed. Return to the saucepan and heat over medium-low heat just until thickened or heated through. Ladle into serving bowls and garnish with thyme or parsley.

Spicy Parmesan Crackers

makes fifty

ingredients

1/2   cup butter
2   cups flour
1 1/2 cups finely grated
      Parmesan cheese
1   large egg yolk
1   teaspoon salt
2   teaspoons ground chipotle pepper
2   teaspoons freshly ground
      black pepper
1/2   cup water

Wonderful with olive tapenade or rich soups.

Pulse the butter in the food processor to chop. Add the flour and process until the mixture resembles coarse meal. Add the cheese and mix well. Add the egg yolk, salt, chipotle pepper and black pepper and mix well.

Add 1/4 cup of the water gradually, processing constantly. Add enough of the remaining water gradually to form a ball. Divide into 2 portions.

Roll 1 portion at a time to 1/4-inch thickness between waxed paper or parchment or on a floured surface. Cut into 1x2-inch squares. Place on ungreased baking sheets and prick several times with a fork.

Bake at 350 degrees for 8 to 10 minutes or until light brown. Turn the crackers and bake for 4 minutes longer or until evenly golden brown. Cool on the baking sheet on a wire rack. Store in an airtight container.

Honey-Soy Dressing

serves eight

ingredients

1/4   cup honey
4   teaspoons soy sauce
2   tablespoons rice wine vinegar

Combine the honey, soy sauce and rice wine vinegar in a bowl and mix well. Serve over a salad of mixed field greens and orange sections.

Pesto Pork

ingredients

6   cups fresh basil leaves
1 1/2 cups grated Parmesan cheese
1   cup pine nuts, toasted
6   (or more) medium garlic cloves
1   tablespoon fresh lemon juice
•   salt and pepper to taste
3/4   cup (or more) olive oil
4   pork tenderloins

When time is at a premium, prepare this with a commercial pesto.

Combine the basil, cheese, pine nuts, garlic, lemon juice, salt and pepper in a food processor and process until smooth. Add enough olive oil gradually to achieve the desired consistency, processing constantly until almost smooth.

Pat the pork dry with paper towels and make 3 long cuts along 1 side of each tenderloin. Sprinkle with salt and pepper. Spread the cut sides with the pesto. Arrange the tenderloins in pairs with the pesto in the center, placing the larger ends opposite the smaller ends; tie securely with string. Rub any remaining pesto over the outside.

Place in a roasting pan and insert a meat thermometer in the thickest portion. Roast at 400 degrees for 45 minutes or to 150 degrees on the meat thermometer. Slice and serve with Gingered Plum Sauce (page 124).

Note: *The pesto sauce may be stored in the refrigerator for up to 1 week or in the freezer for up to 6 months.*

Gingered Plum Sauce

serves eight

ingredients

2   cups unsweetened plum jam
1/3   cup apple cider vinegar
1/3   cup packed brown sugar
1/2   cup port
2   tablespoons grated gingerroot
•   juice of 2 lemons
I   teaspoon ground cloves
I   teaspoon nutmeg
•   salt and pepper to taste

This is best made with unsweetened plum jam. Use slightly less brown sugar if the jam is sweetened.

Combine the plum jam, vinegar, brown sugar, wine, gingerroot, lemon juice, cloves, nutmeg, salt and pepper in a medium saucepan. Simmer over low heat for 30 minutes. Cool to room temperature.

Process the mixture in a food processor until smooth. Return to the saucepan and cook just until heated through.

Steamed Bok Choy

serves eight

ingredients

2   pounds baby bok choy
1/4   teaspoon salt
•   white pepper to taste
2   tablespoons fresh lemon juice

Bring the water in a steamer to a boil and add the bok choy. Steam over high heat for 2 minutes. Sprinkle with the salt and white pepper. Steam for 2 minutes longer. Sprinkle with the lemon juice to serve.

Note: *If you cannot find baby bok choy, cut a large stalk into halves lengthwise and then into halves crosswise. Steam the stem half for 2 minutes, add the leaves and steam for 2 minutes longer.*

Pears in Red Wine

ingredients

1	cup fine sugar
1^1/$_3$	cups red wine
3	cinnamon sticks
1	strip of lemon peel
8	Bosc pears
1	tablespoon Cointreau
•	sliced almonds (optional)

Dissolve the sugar in the wine in a saucepan over low heat. Add the cinnamon sticks and lemon peel. Boil the mixture until it forms a thin syrup.

Peel the pears, leaving the stems intact. Place upright in the syrup. Simmer for 1 hour or until tender. Remove the pears to a serving dish, reserving the syrup. Boil the syrup until reduced by half; discard the cinnamon sticks and lemon peel.

Stir the liqueur into the syrup. Pour over the pears and sprinkle with almonds. Chill until serving time, spooning the syrup over the pears occasionally. Serve cold.

for eight
MAJOR COMPOSITION

when the lights went out in georgia

Years ago we were playing an evening concert in Cedartown, Georgia, and we had a substitute second trombone player. While we were playing *Capriccio espagnol*, the lights went out during a thunderstorm. The orchestra had played the piece many times before, so we just kept playing in the dark. Not knowing this, the poor trombone player heard everybody playing along and thought something had happened to his eyes. We played for a minute or so, and then everybody slowly fizzled out. By then the trombone player was absolutely white as a ghost!

Joe Walthall, Trumpet

wild mushroom SOUP

WARM *goat cheese* ON GREENS

washington state pinot noir

ROSEMARY-ROASTED *prime rib*

WINTER *white purée*

STEAMED *haricots verts*

robust california red zinfandel

cranberry COBBLER WITH *walnut cream*

ruby port

Wild Mushroom Soup

serves eight

ingredients

1¹/2 pounds mixed fresh wild
    mushrooms such as oyster,
    portobello or cremini
1¹/2 pounds button mushrooms
¹/4 cup chopped fresh thyme
¹/4 cup chopped fresh tarragon
• kosher salt to taste
3 tablespoons extra-virgin olive oil
1 cup minced shallots
1¹/2 quarts chicken stock, preferably
    homemade
³/4 cup dry sherry
1¹/2 cups heavy cream
1 teaspoon crushed red pepper
• freshly ground black pepper
    to taste

garnish

• sprigs of fresh tarragon
• crème frâiche

Wipe the mushrooms and separate the stems and caps of the wild mushrooms; reserve the caps. Combine the wild mushroom stems, button mushrooms and half the fresh herbs in a food processor and pulse several times to chop. Add kosher salt to taste.

Combine the minced mushrooms, olive oil, shallots and chicken stock in a skillet. Bring to a boil over medium heat and reduce the heat. Simmer for 10 minutes or until the mushrooms have shrunk to half their volume. Add ¹/2 cup of the sherry and simmer for 10 minutes longer. Cool for 15 minutes. Pour into a strainer over a saucepan and press to remove all the liquid; discard the pulp.

Slice or tear the reserved mushroom caps into bite-size pieces and add to the liquid in the saucepan. Add the cream, remaining herbs and red pepper. Simmer until the soup thickens slightly. Add the remaining ¹/4 cup sherry and simmer for 2 to 3 minutes longer. Correct the seasoning with salt and black pepper. Ladle into warmed soup bowls and garnish with sprigs of fresh tarragon or a swirl of crème frâiche.

Note: *If fresh wild mushrooms are not available, substitute 2 ounces of dried wild mushroom, rehydrated, and double the amount of button mushrooms, reserving 3 ounces of the button mushrooms to add to the strained stock.*

Rosemary-Roasted Prime Rib

serves eight

ingredients

1   (6-pound) prime rib of beef
1/4   cup olive oil
15   garlic cloves, chopped
1/2   cup rosemary leaves
•   salt to taste
1 1/2 tablespoons pepper

Rub the prime rib with some of the olive oil and sprinkle with the garlic, rosemary, salt and pepper, pressing to coat well. Drizzle with the remaining olive oil. Place rib side down on a rack in a roasting pan. Insert a meat thermometer in the thickest portion of the meat.

Roast at 350 degrees until the meat thermometer registers rare; cover with foil if necessary to prevent overbrowning. Let stand for 15 minutes before carving.

Warm Goat Cheese on Greens

serves eight

ingredients

2   small logs of goat cheese, chilled
1/4   to 1/2 cup flour
•   mixed field greens
•   Roasted Tomato Vinaigrette (page 97) or other vinaigrette

Slice the goat cheese into rounds. Coat well with the flour. Spray a skillet with nonstick cooking spray and heat over medium heat. Add the cheese and pan-fry until golden brown.

Place the field greens on individual serving plates. Top with the goat cheese. Drizzle with vinaigrette.

Note: *The pan-fried cheese may be kept at room temperature for up to 1 hour before serving.*

Winter White Purée

serves eight

ingredients

1	pound white turnips
1	pound parsnips
1	tart green apple
4	quarts water
•	salt to taste
8	ounces cauliflowerets
10	tablespoons unsalted butter, sliced
3/4	cup heavy cream
•	freshly ground white pepper to taste
1/2	cup freshly grated Parmesan cheese

Peel the turnips, parsnips and apple and cut into 1-inch pieces. Bring the water to a boil in a saucepan. Add salt to taste, cauliflowerets, chopped vegetables and apple. Cook for 15 minutes or until fork tender; drain.

Process the mixture in a food processor or potato ricer until puréed. Add the butter gradually, processing until smooth. Add the cream and pulse to mix well. Season with salt and white pepper.

Spoon into a buttered 2-quart baking dish; smooth the top and sprinkle with the cheese. Bake at 350 degrees for 20 minutes or until light brown.

Note: *The purée may be prepared one day in advance and stored in the refrigerator. Let stand until room temperature and bake as above.*

Cranberry Cobbler with Walnut Cream

serves eight

walnut cream

I cup whipping cream
I tablespoon sugar
I teaspoon vanilla extract
1/4 cup finely chopped walnuts

cranberry filling

4 1/2 cups fresh cranberries
2/3 cup sugar
I tablespoon flour
I tablespoon finely grated
    orange zest
2 teaspoons cinnamon
I teaspoon nutmeg

biscuit topping

1 1/2 cups flour
3 tablespoons sugar
2 1/4 teaspoons baking powder
2 teaspoons finely grated
    orange zest
2 teaspoons cinnamon
1/2 teaspoon cardamom
1/2 teaspoon kosher salt
6 tablespoons unsalted butter,
    chilled, cut into 1/2-inch pieces
3/4 cup heavy cream
I tablespoon sugar

For the walnut cream, beat the whipping cream in a bowl with a hand mixer until soft peaks form. Add the sugar and vanilla gradually, beating until the peaks hold their shape. Fold in the walnuts. Chill until serving time.

For the filling, combine the cranberries, sugar, flour, orange zest, cinnamon and nutmeg in a bowl and mix lightly. Spoon into a 1 1/2-quart baking dish.

For the topping, mix the flour, 3 tablespoons sugar, baking powder, orange zest, cinnamon, cardamom and salt in a bowl. Cut in the butter until the mixture resembled coarse crumbs. Add the cream and mix just until the mixture forms a soft dough.

Shape into biscuits 2 to 2 1/2 inches in diameter and 1/2 inch thick. Arrange over the cranberries. Sprinkle with I tablespoon sugar.

Bake at 375 degrees for 30 to 40 minutes or until bubbly and golden brown. Serve with the walnut cream.

RHAPSODY IN DINING

shaw-isms

The members of the Atlanta Symphony Orchestra Chorus shared a collective and abiding love and respect for Robert Shaw. They also respected his ability to nail a choral weakness with a well-turned phrase. The following comments were collected by Charlie Cottingham, long-time Symphony Chorus member.

"This is cleanliness, but it's a long way from Godliness."

"As long as you're that close to B-flat, you might as well sing it. He wrote it and it's been there a long time."

"If the piano weren't playing that G-sharp, we wouldn't have it anywhere in the room."

"It's marked *pianissimo*, and all of a sudden you sing *mezzo-forte belcho!*"

POTATO *pancake with* SMOKED *salmon*

pinot blanc alsace

VIDALIA *onion tart*

german riesling kabinett

ROASTED *sturgeon* WITH *moscato sauerkraut* AND GLAZED *grapes*

gewürtztraminer

honey parfait WITH HONEY CRISP AND BLOOD ORANGE CONFIT

moscato di asti

FROM *Seeger's*

Potato Pancake with Smoked Salmon

serves six

ingredients

1	pound potatoes, chopped, cooked
1/4	cup potato starch
3	egg yolks
1	cup heavy cream
3	egg whites
•	salt and pepper to taste
8	ounces clarified butter
•	smoked salmon

garnish

- fresh dill sprigs or tiny lettuce leaves

Combine the potatoes, potato starch, egg yolks and cream in a medium bowl and mix with a wooden spoon or spatula until smooth. Beat the egg whites in a mixing bowl until stiff peaks form. Fold into the potato mixture. Season with salt and pepper. Spoon into a pastry bag.

Heat 6 tablespoons butter in a medium skillet over medium heat. Pipe about 2 ounces of the potato mixture at a time into the skillet. Cook until bubbles appear on the top and turn the pancake carefully. Cook until golden brown; drain on paper towels. Continue with the remaining potato mixture, adding additional butter as needed.

Arrange the pancakes in the centers of serving plates and top with the smoked salmon. Garnish with dill or lettuce.

Vidalia Onion Tart

tart crust

2   cups plus 1 tablespoon flour
•   pinch of salt
10   tablespoons butter, chilled, chopped
1/4   cup cold water

vidalia onion filling

3   Vidalia onions, chopped
2   tablespoons butter
1   cup heavy cream
1   egg
1   egg yolk
•   freshly grated nutmeg to taste
•   salt and pepper to taste
1   tablespoon sautéed finely minced bacon
•   cumin seeds to taste

For the crust, combine the flour and salt in a bowl. Add the butter and work into the dry ingredients with the fingers. Add the water and mix just enough to form a dough; do not overmix. Chill for 2 hours or longer. Roll the dough 1/8 inch thick on a floured surface. Fit into a tart pan and prick well with a fork.

For the filling, sauté the onions in the butter in a saucepan just until tender. Add the cream and cook until thickened and reduced; remove from the heat. Add the egg and egg yolk and mix well. Season with nutmeg, salt and pepper.

Spoon into the prepared tart pan and sprinkle with the bacon and cumin seeds. Bake at 450 degrees on bottom oven rack for 20 to 25 minutes or until golden brown.

134   SOUNDS DELICIOUS

Roasted Sturgeon with Moscato Sauerkraut

glazed grapes

3	tablespoons butter
1	tablespoon sugar
1/4	cup white wine
30	grapes, peeled

moscato sauerkraut

1	shallot, chopped
•	butter
2	pounds sauerkraut
1/4	liter Moscato
1/2	Granny Smith apple, peeled, grated
1/4	Yukon gold potato, peeled, grated
•	salt and pepper to taste

sturgeon

1	(3-pound) sturgeon fillet, skinned
10	sage leaves
1	pound thinly sliced bacon

For the grapes, combine the butter, sugar and white wine in a saucepan and mix well. Cook to 300 degrees on a candy thermometer, hard-crack stage. Place over hot water. Dip the grapes into the mixture, coating completely. Place on a wire rack to cool.

For the sauerkraut, sauté the shallot in a small amount of butter in a saucepan until very tender. Add the sauerkraut and Moscato and cook for 10 minutes. Stir in the apple and potato and cook for 5 minutes longer. Season with salt and pepper.

For the sturgeon, cover the fish with the sage leaves and wrap with bacon. Place in a roasting pan. Roast at 450 degrees for 5 minutes on each side. Remove to a warm plate and let rest for 5 minutes.

Spoon the sauerkraut into the center of a serving plate. Place the sturgeon over the sauerkraut and arrange the grapes around the edge.

Honey Parfait

ingredients

1   quart whipping cream
3¹/₂ egg yolks
•   seeds of 1 vanilla bean
200   grams organic honey
1   tablespoon Grand Marnier
1   recipe Honey Crisp (page 137)
1   recipe Blood Orange Confit
      (page 137)

Whip the cream in a mixing bowl until soft peaks form. Combine the egg yolks, vanilla bean seeds and honey in a mixing bowl until thickened and pale yellow. Fold into the whipped cream. Fold in the Grand Marnier.

Spoon into a loaf pan. Freeze until firm. Unmold the parfait onto a plate. Cut into 10 slices. Place 1 slice of Honey Crisp on each side of each parfait slice. Stand on serving plates. Spoon the Blood Orange Confit around the parfait.

Honey Crisp

ingredients

40   grams butter, softened
67.5 grams confectioners' sugar
•   seeds of $^1/_2$ vanilla bean
45   grams honey
$1^1/_2$ egg whites
65   grams flour

Cream the butter in a mixing bowl until light and fluffy. Add the confectioners' sugar, vanilla bean seeds and honey and mix well. Beat in the egg whites and flour.

Spoon into a loaf pan. Bake at 330 degrees until golden brown. Cool in the pan for several minutes; invert onto a wire rack to cool completely. Cut into 20 slices when cool.

Blood Orange Confit

ingredients

•   grated zest of 5 blood oranges
$^1/_2$ tablespoon arrowroot
250   ml white wine
50   grams confectioners' sugar
$^1/_2$ vanilla bean
•   sections of 5 blood oranges

Blanch the orange zest in boiling water in a saucepan; drain. Dissolve the arrowroot in a small amount of the white wine in a bowl.

Combine the remaining wine, confectioners' sugar and vanilla bean in a saucepan. Cook until the alcohol evaporates. Add the arrowroot mixture and cook until thickened, stirring constantly.

Pour over the orange sections and orange zest in a bowl and mix lightly. Chill, covered with plastic wrap, until serving time.

ON THE GRAND SCALE
COCKTAILS AND BUFFETS

the menus

Cocktail Cantabile
Buffet Fantasia
Up-Tempo Entertaining

the music

Beethoven: Overtures
Telarc CD-80358

Bach: B-Minor Mass
Telarc CD-80233

"Grand and Glorious: Great Opera Choruses"
Telarc CD-80333

Copland: Symphony No. 3/Music for the Theatre
Telarc CD-80201

COCKTAIL CANTABILE

ringside at the nutcracker

Before the Woodruff Arts Center became its home, the Atlanta Symphony played concerts in the Municipal Auditorium, a multi-use venue downtown which was also used for a variety of other events such as wrestling matches. Nancy Burke, then in charge of the Symphony's ticket sales, was working in the Box Office during the orchestra's annual appearance with the Atlanta Ballet in Tchaikovsky's *Nutcracker*. A man, dressed in overalls and with brown bag in hand, inquired, "Who's on tonight?" "*The Nutcracker*," Nancy replied. The man said, "Never heard of him, but I'll take a ringside seat on the name only!"

Nola Frink, Choral Administrator

SMOKED *salmon canapés*

polenta triangles WITH SUN-DRIED TOMATO *pesto*

stuffed PATTYPAN *squash*

CHICKEN LIVER *pâté*

CARAMELIZED *endive and pear tart*

vintage french champagne
full bar

Smoked Salmon Canapés serves sixteen

ingredients

1   cup unsalted butter, softened
1   (8-ounce) can salmon
6   or 7 ounces smoked salmon, chopped
•   Tabasco sauce to taste
•   minced fresh dill to taste
•   salt and pepper to taste
3   to 4 tablespoons vodka
•   thinly sliced rye bread, crusts trimmed

garnish

•   tiny sprigs of dill

Beat the butter in a mixer bowl until light. Drain the canned salmon, discarding the skin and bones. Combine with the smoked salmon in the food processor and process until smooth. Add the butter, Tabasco sauce, dill, salt and pepper and mix well. Adjust the seasonings and add the vodka; mix well.

Spoon into a covered container and chill until serving time. Spread on the rye bread and garnish with dill sprigs. Cover with plastic wrap until time to serve.

Polenta Triangles with Sun-Dried Tomato Pesto serves sixteen

ingredients

1   package polenta
•   pesto (page 123)
1/2 cup drained sun-dried tomatoes or cherry tomatoes

Prepare the polenta using the package directions; spread 1/2 inch thick in a shallow dish. Chill in the refrigerator for 2 hours or longer. Cut into small triangles.

Brown the triangles in a nonstick skillet sprayed with nonstick cooking spray. Spread with the pesto and top with a tomato.

Stuffed Pattypan Squash

ingredients

16 small pattypan squash
8   ounces bleu cheese, crumbled
6   ounces shredded sharp
    Cheddar cheese
•   red or black pepper to taste
    (optional)
•   grated lemon zest to taste
    (optional)

Small pattypan or turban squash can be found in gourmet markets. Substitute one-inch slices of yellow squash or zucchini if the pattypan are not available.

Steam the squash in a steamer for 7 minutes or until tender. Drain and cool completely. Cut off the tops of the squashes and scoop out some of the pulp.

Combine the bleu cheese and Cheddar cheese in a small bowl and mix with hands. Season with the pepper and lemon zest. Spoon into the squashes.

Place on a baking sheet. Broil for 5 minutes or just until the cheese melts. Serve immediately.

Stuffed Pattypan Squash / Polenta Triangles with Sun-Dried Tomato Pesto on page 141

Chicken Liver Pâté

ingredients

1	pound chicken livers
4	large shallots, chopped
2	garlic cloves, minced
6	tablespoons unsalted butter
1/2	cup chopped green onions
1/4	cup chopped fresh basil
1	tablespoon chopped fresh parsley
3	tablespoons (or more) cognac
1	tablespoon balsamic vinegar
1	tablespoon cider vinegar
1	tablespoon dry mustard
1/4	teaspoon nutmeg
1	tablespoon salt
4	ounces cream cheese, softened

garnish

1	tablespoon chopped fresh parsley

Sauté the chicken livers with the shallots and garlic in the butter in a large skillet over medium heat for 4 to 5 minutes. Add the green onions, basil, parsley, cognac, balsamic vinegar, cider vinegar, dry mustard, nutmeg and salt. Cook over medium-high heat for 2 minutes. Remove from the heat and cool for 5 minutes.

Combine with the cream cheese in a food processor container and process until smooth. Add additional cognac if desired. Spoon into a serving bowl or small ramekins. Chill, covered, for 8 hours or longer. Garnish with parsley.

Serve with warm bread, apples, grapes and assorted cheeses.

Caramelized Endive and Pear Tart

serves sixteen

ingredients

2	heads Belgian endive, chopped
1/2	cup chopped shallots
2	teaspoons dried oregano
2	tablespoons unsalted butter
3	large pears, peeled, chopped
1	tablespoon balsamic vinegar
1	cup Stilton cheese, crumbled
3	tablespoons chopped chives
2	sheets frozen puff pastry, thawed
1	large egg, lightly beaten

Keep the pastry cold while preparing the tart to prevent holes from developing and allowing the filling to seep out as it cooks.

Sauté the endive and shallots with the oregano in the butter in a large heavy skillet over medium-high heat for 8 minutes or until the endive is golden brown. Add the pears and vinegar and cook for 2 minutes or until the pears are tender. Remove to a bowl and cool. Stir in the cheese and chives.

Roll the pastry sheets into larger rectangles on a lightly floured surface. Place 1 sheet on a heavy baking sheet sprayed with nonstick cooking spray; refrigerate the remaining pastry. Brush with the egg, brushing to the edges of the pastry.

Spread the endive mixture over the pastry, leaving a 1/2-inch border. Top with the remaining pastry, pressing the edges to seal. Brush with the egg. Chill in the refrigerator or freeze for 10 minutes.

Bake the tart at 425 degrees for 25 minutes or until puffed and golden brown. Let stand for 1 hour before serving. Cut into wedges or squares to serve.

Note: *This can also be prepared as bite-size tartlets if desired.*

BUFFET FANTASIA

running an olympic sprint

During the Opening Ceremony of the 1996 Olympics, the entire chorus stood together and sang the National Anthem. Our next piece required several of the chorus members to sing from the far end of the stadium. As the National Anthem ended, two groups peeled off, ran around and underneath the stadium to the far end, climbed all the way up, and stood at the top. My group barely made it in time; as we were running around, President Clinton was going back to his seat, and the Secret Service made us wait until he was seated.

Ellen Dukes, Symphony Chorus Member

BASIL *cheese terrine*

SPICED *pecans*

SMOKED *salmon bruschetta* WITH TOMATO-AVOCADO SALSA

FRUIT-INFUSED *turkey* WITH JEZEBEL SAUCE

persimmon MUFFINS • MINIATURE *rolls*

SANTA FE *chicken pizzas*

SMOKED GOUDA *quesadillas*

COCONUT *macaroons*

SICILIAN *reginas*

CARAMEL ALMOND *cashew bars*

full bar
american sparkling wines
chilled microbrew and imported beers

Basil Cheese Terrine

serves sixteen

ingredients

8	ounces cream cheese, softened
4	ounces bleu cheese, crumbled
1	cup loosely packed spinach leaves
3/4	cup loosely packed parsley leaves
1/4	cup loosely packed basil leaves
2	garlic cloves, minced
1/4	teaspoon salt
1/4	cup olive oil
1/4	cup chopped pine nuts
1	cup grated Parmesan cheese
1/2	cup oil-pack sun-dried tomatoes, drained, sliced

garnish

- fresh basil sprigs
- cherry tomato wedges

Process the cream cheese and bleu cheese in the food processor until smooth. Spoon into a small bowl and set aside.

Combine the spinach, parsley, basil, garlic and salt in a food processor container and process until smooth. Add the olive oil gradually, processing constantly. Combine with the pine nuts and Parmesan cheese in a bowl and mix well.

Line a 3x7-inch loaf pan with plastic wrap, allowing enough overhang to cover the terrine. Spread half the cheese mixture in the prepared pan. Add layers of half the sun-dried tomatoes, the spinach mixture, the remaining tomatoes and the remaining cheese mixture. Cover with the plastic wrap.

Chill for 24 hours. Let stand at room temperature for 30 minutes. Uncover the terrine and invert onto a serving platter; discard the plastic wrap. Garnish with basil sprigs and cherry tomato wedges. Serve with crackers and breadsticks.

Spiced Pecans

makes two cups

ingredients

2	tablespoons butter
1	tablespoon olive oil
1	tablespoon Worcestershire sauce
1/2	teaspoon Tabasco sauce
3/4	teaspoon ground cumin
1/2	teaspoon paprika
1/2	teaspoon garlic powder
2	cups pecan halves
2	teaspoons coarse salt (optional)

Melt the butter in the olive oil in a saucepan. Add the Worcestershire sauce, Tabasco sauce, cumin, paprika and garlic powder and simmer for 2 to 3 minutes. Stir in the pecan halves. Spread on a baking sheet and bake at 325 degrees for 15 minutes, stirring occasionally. Toss with the salt. Cool on the baking sheet and store in an airtight container.

Smoked Salmon Bruschetta with Tomato-Avocado Salsa

Smoked Salmon Bruschetta with Tomato-Avocado Salsa   serves sixteen

tomato-avocado salsa

3	small plum tomatoes, chopped
1	small yellow bell pepper, chopped
3	tablespoons chopped red onion, with juices
1	small jalapeño pepper, chopped
1	small avocado, chopped
3	tablespoons finely chopped fresh basil
1	tablespoon fresh lime juice
1	teaspoon olive oil
•	salt and pepper to taste

bruschetta

1	medium baguette
2	large garlic cloves, peeled, cut into halves
•	olive oil
•	salt and pepper to taste
4	ounces thinly sliced smoked salmon
•	olive oil
•	salt and pepper to taste

For the salsa, combine the tomatoes, bell pepper, onion, jalapeño pepper, avocado, basil, lime juice and olive oil in a bowl. Season with salt and pepper and mix well. Let stand for 15 minutes or longer to blend flavors.

For the bruschetta, slice the baguette into $1/2$-inch slices and arrange on a large baking sheet. Toast at 350 degrees for 3 minutes or until slightly crisp. Rub both sides of each slice of bread with the garlic. Drizzle each side with about 1 teaspoon olive oil and sprinkle with salt and pepper. Return to the oven and toast just until light brown. Cool to room temperature.

Arrange the bread slices on a serving platter. Place a small slice of salmon on each slice of bread and top with the salsa.

Fruit-Infused Turkey

serves sixteen

ingredients

1	(12-ounce) package dried apricots
1	(12-ounce) package pitted dried prunes
1	(12-ounce) package dried apples
3	bay leaves
1	bottle of sherry
1	(10- to 12-pound) turkey
2	cups orange juice
•	salt and pepper to taste

For this recipe, you will need a syringe or food infuser, available at specialty stores for cookware.

Combine the apricots, prunes and apples with the bay leaves and sherry in a large plastic or glass container. Marinate in the refrigerator for 1 to 3 days.

Strain the mixture several times through a very fine strainer or cheesecloth to remove any particles; reserve the liquid and the fruit, discarding the bay leaves. Fill the syringe with the reserved liquid.

Rub the outside of the turkey with the orange juice. Inject the fruit liquid into the turkey. Stuff the cavity of the turkey with the reserved fruit. Season with salt and pepper. Truss the turkey and place in a roasting pan; tent lightly with foil.

Roast using the instructions with the turkey, removing the foil tent toward the end of the roasting time to brown the turkey.

Let the turkey stand until it can be thinly sliced to serve with Persimmon Muffins (page 151) and Jezebel Sauce made by stirring spicy mustard into pineapple preserves.

Note: *The turkey will be brown on the outside and very moist and flavorful on the inside. The meat will be discolored from the infusion, similar to smoked turkey. Marinated fruit is delicious added to your favorite stuffing recipe.*

Persimmon Muffins

ingredients

2	large or 4 small very ripe persimmons, peeled
1	teaspoon baking soda
3	cups flour
1	cup sugar
4	teaspoons baking powder
1	teaspoon cinnamon
1	teaspoon nutmeg
1/2	teaspoon ground cloves
1	teaspoon salt
1	cup golden raisins
2	eggs
1	cup milk
1/2	cup melted butter
2	teaspoon grated lemon zest

Press the persimmons through a colander or food mill; do not process in a blender. Measure 1 cup of the pulp. Combine with the baking soda in a bowl and mix well.

Sift the flour, sugar, baking powder, cinnamon, nutmeg, cloves and salt into a large bowl. Add the raisins and toss to coat well.

Beat the eggs in a medium bowl. Add the milk, butter, lemon zest and persimmon pulp and mix well. Add to the flour mixture and mix just until moistened; batter will be lumpy.

Spoon into greased medium muffin cups, filling 2/3 full. Bake at 400 degrees for 15 to 18 minutes or until golden brown.

Miniature Rolls

ingredients

1/2	cup butter or margarine, softened
1	cup self-rising flour
1/2	cup sour cream

Beat the butter with the flour in a bowl until smooth. Add the sour cream and mix well. Drop by spoonfuls into greased miniature muffin cups, filling the cups. Bake at 400 degrees for 20 to 25 minutes or until golden brown.

Santa Fe Chicken Pizzas

grilled lime chicken

1	tablespoon fresh lime juice
$1/2$	teaspoon Worcestershire sauce
$1^1/2$	teaspoons soy sauce
$1/2$	teaspoon honey
1	tablespoon chopped fresh cilantro
2	tablespoons olive oil
•	cumin and red pepper flakes to taste
2	(5-ounce) boneless skinless chicken breasts

caramelized onions

$1^1/2$	tablespoons unsalted butter
1	large yellow or purple onion, sliced into $1/8$-inch rings
$1/4$	teaspoon red wine vinegar
1	teaspoon soy sauce

pizzas

•	pizza dough for 2 (9-inch) pizzas
2	cups shredded mozzarella cheese

garnish

2	tablespoons chopped fresh cilantro

Increase this recipe to make as many pizzas as needed for your crowd.

For the chicken, combine the lime juice, Worcestershire sauce, soy sauce, honey, cilantro, olive oil, cumin and red pepper flakes in a bowl and mix well. Add the chicken and marinate for 15 minutes or longer.

Drain the chicken, discarding the marinade. Grill over hot coals for 5 to 7 minutes on each side. Chill in the refrigerator. Cut into $1/2$-inch pieces and chill until needed.

For the onions, melt the butter in a small nonstick skillet over medium-high heat. Add the onions and cook for 3 to 4 minutes or just until they begin to brown. Add the vinegar and reduce the heat to medium-low. Cook for 10 minutes, stirring constantly. Add the soy sauce and cook for 5 to 10 minutes longer or until brown, stirring constantly.

For the pizzas, spread the onions over the pizza dough. Top each with $3/4$ cup of the cheese and sprinkle with the chicken. Add the remaining cheese.

Bake at 475 degrees for 8 to 10 minutes or until the cheese is bubbly and the crust is golden brown. Garnish with the cilantro. Cut into wedges and serve with chunky salsa, sour cream and guacamole.

Smoked Gouda Quesadillas makes four

ingredients

1	purple onion, coarsely chopped
2	tablespoons butter
3	tablespoons brown sugar
1	tablespoon balsamic vinegar
2	tablespoons canola oil
8	small flour tortillas
8	ounces (or more) smoked gouda cheese, sliced

Increase the recipe to make enough quesadillas to serve your party.

Sweat the onion in the butter in a large skillet over medium heat until tender. Add the brown sugar and cook until the sugar begins to caramelize, stirring constantly. Stir in the vinegar. Cook until the onion is brown.

Heat 1 tablespoon oil at a time in a skillet. Add 2 tortillas and cook just until heated. Add $1/4$ of the cheese and onion to each tortilla and top with a second tortilla; press with a spatula. Cook until golden brown, turning several times. Repeat with the remaining ingredients.

Cut into wedges and serve hot with sour cream and salsa.

Coconut Macaroons

makes five dozen

ingredients

2²/3 cups sweetened coconut
1/2 cup flour
1/2 cup sugar
4 egg whites
1/4 cup sugar
1 teaspoon vanilla extract
1/4 cup heavy cream
2 tablespoons unsalted butter
1/2 teaspoon grated orange zest
6 ounces semisweet chocolate

Chop the coconut in the food processor. Combine with the flour and 1/2 cup sugar in a bowl.

Beat the egg whites in a mixing bowl until soft peaks form. Add 1/4 cup sugar and beat for 1 minute. Add the vanilla and beat until peaks hold their shape. Fold into the coconut mixture.

Shape into small balls and arrange 1 inch apart on a parchment-covered cookie sheet. Bake at 325 degrees for 20 minutes or until light brown. Cool on a wire rack.

Combine the cream, butter and orange zest in a saucepan and bring to a simmer; reduce the heat to low. Add the chocolate and stir until smooth. Let stand for 30 minutes.

Dip the top halves of the macaroons into the chocolate. Place on waxed paper and let stand until set.

Caramel Almond Cashew Bars

makes eight dozen

ingredients

1 1/2 cups butter, softened
2/3 cup sugar
2 1/2 teaspoons grated lemon zest
3 cups flour
1/2 cup cornstarch
1/2 teaspoon salt
10 tablespoons butter
1/2 cup packed brown sugar
1/3 cup honey
1 1/2 cups whole almonds
1 1/2 cups salted cashews
2 1/2 tablespoons heavy cream

Cream 1 1/2 cups butter and sugar in a mixing bowl until light and fluffy. Beat in the lemon zest. Sift the flour, cornstarch and salt together. Add to the creamed mixture gradually, mixing well after each addition.

Press into a foil-lined 9x13-inch baking pan, shaping edges 1 inch high. Prick all over with a fork. Bake at 350 degrees for 40 minutes, pricking any areas that begin to puff up.

Combine 10 tablespoons butter, brown sugar and honey in a heavy saucepan. Cook until the butter melts, stirring to blend well. Cook until the mixture thickens without stirring. Remove from the heat and stir in the almonds, cashews and cream.

Spread over the baked layer. Bake for 20 minutes longer. Cool in the pan on a wire rack and cut into small squares.

Sicilian Reginas

ingredients

1/4	cup butter, softened
1/2	cup sugar
I	large egg yolk
3/4	teaspoon vanilla extract
1/4	teaspoon almond extract
1/4	cup milk
3/4	cup all-purpose flour
I	cup cake flour
1/4	teaspoon baking powder
2	large egg whites
1/2	cup sesame seeds

These semisweet little cookies are similar to biscotti, but they have a delicious nutty sesame seed coating. They are wonderful with coffee or tea, or with an after-dinner drink.

Cream the butter in a mixing bowl until light. Add the sugar and beat until fluffy. Beat in the egg yolk and flavorings. Add the milk and mix well.

Mix the all-purpose flour, cake flour and baking powder together. Add to the creamed mixture and mix to form a dough. Knead lightly on a floured surface. Divide into 24 portions and roll each portion to form a 2-inch log.

Whisk the egg whites until frothy in a small bowl. Place the sesame seeds in a shallow dish. Dip each log into the egg whites and coat with the sesame seeds. Arrange 1 inch apart on a cookie sheet.

Bake at 350 degrees for 12 minutes or just until set but not brown. Remove to a wire rack to cool.

UP-TEMPO ENTERTAINING

score one for violins

At one concert, Mr. Shaw came out, bowed, and started conducting. As the orchestra started to play, he looked down at the score and realized it was the wrong music! He kept conducting, but he looked up, indicated for me to come to the podium, and told me that he had the wrong score. So while the orchestra was still playing and wondering what in the world I was doing, and the audience was wondering if something was wrong with Mr. Shaw, I walked off the stage, retrieved the correct score, gave it to Mr. Shaw, sat back down, and played on as if nothing had happened.

Dave Arenz, Principal Second Violin
Atlanta Symphony Associates Chair

WARM GRILLED *vegetable salad*
WITH PESTO KALAMATA *vinaigrette*

SMOKED *salmon* AND CIPOLLINI *cheesecake*
WITH SHERRY DILL *crème frâiche*
AND PEPPERCORN PARMESAN *pita chips*

ROSEMARY-STUDDED *quail*
WITH *fig* CHANTERELLE *stuffing*
AND ORANGE AND *port gastrique*

ASIAN *duck and* SOBA *noodle salad*
WITH LEMON GRASS *vinaigrette*

LOBSTER AND ASPARAGUS *risotto cakes*
AND POMODORO *sauce*

white chocolate GRAND MARNIER *torte*

full cocktail service
freshly brewed colombian coffee

FROM *Legendary Events*

Warm Grilled Vegetable Salad with Pesto Kalamata Vinaigrette
serves ten

pesto kalamata vinaigrette

1/3	cup pesto
1	tablespoon sugar
1/2	cup white balsamic vinegar
•	salt and white pepper to taste
1 1/2	cups extra-virgin olive oil
1/3	cup julienned kalamata olives

balsamic marinade

1	cup extra-virgin olive oil
1/2	cup white balsamic vinegar
•	salt and pepper to taste

salad

5	Japanese eggplant
3	zucchini
1	large red onion
3	yellow bell peppers
3	red bell peppers
10	Roma tomatoes
1	portobello mushroom
5	(3-ounce) balls buffalo mozzarella, sliced

garnish

1/4	cup chopped fresh opal basil

For the vinaigrette, combine the pesto, sugar, vinegar, salt and white pepper in a blender container and process for 15 seconds. Add the olive oil gradually, blending constantly until smooth. Combine with the olives in a bowl or jar and mix well. Chill until serving time.

For the marinade, combine the olive oil, vinegar, salt and pepper in a large bowl and mix well.

For the salad, slice the eggplant and zucchini diagonally 1/2 inch thick. Slice the onion and bell peppers 1/4 inch thick. Slice the tomatoes 1/2 inch thick. Add the sliced vegetables and the mushroom to the marinade and mix well. Marinate for 5 minutes.

Grill the vegetables until tender crisp. Arrange on a serving platter and top with the cheese and vinaigrette. Garnish with basil.

Smoked Salmon and Cipollini Cheesecake

serves twenty-five

ingredients

1	pound sliced pepper-crusted smoked salmon
4	(4-ounce) smoked trout fillets
$^1/_2$	cup heavy cream, at room temperature
12	cipollini onions, julienned
1	teaspoon minced garlic
1	fennel bulb, finely chopped
1	red bell pepper, finely chopped
•	dill to taste
$^1/_4$	cup butter
•	Tabasco sauce to taste
40	ounces cream cheese, softened
3	large eggs
$^3/_4$	cup heavy cream

Cipollini onions, the bulbs of the grape hyacinth, are sometimes called wild onions. They can be found in Italian markets.

Line the bottom of a buttered springform pan with half the smoked salmon slices and half the trout fillets. Combine the remaining salmon and trout with $^1/_2$ cup cream in the food processor or blender container and process until smooth.

Sauté the onions, garlic, fennel, bell pepper and dill in the butter in a skillet until tender. Season with Tabasco sauce.

Combine the cream cheese, eggs, $^3/_4$ cup cream, sautéed vegetables and fish purée in a mixing bowl. Mix for 5 to 10 minutes or until completely smooth. Pour into the prepared springform pan.

Place the springform pan in a large pan of water. Bake at 350 degrees for $1^1/_4$ hours or until a wooden pick inserted in the center comes out clean. Cool on a wire rack. Chill in the refrigerator. Place on a serving plate and remove the side of the pan.

Serve with Sherry Dill Crème Frâiche and Peppercorn Parmesan Pita Chips (page 159).

Sherry Dill Crème Fraîche

makes two and one-half cups

ingredients

2   tablespoons finely chopped
    shallots
1   cup sherry
1   tablespoon lemon juice
3   tablespoons finely chopped
    fresh dill
1   tablespoon Old Bay seasoning
•   Tabasco sauce to taste
2   cups crème frâiche
•   salt to taste

Cook the shallots in the sherry in a saucepan until the mixture is reduced by 2/3. Cool to room temperature.

Combine the lemon juice, dill, Old Bay seasoning, Tabasco sauce and crème frâiche in a bowl and mix well. Stir in the shallot mixture and salt to taste. Store in the refrigerator for 1 day or longer to blend flavors.

Peppercorn Parmesan Pita Chips

makes four dozen

ingredients

3   pita bread rounds
1/2 cup melted butter
1   teaspoon paprika
1   teaspoon freshly ground pink
     peppercorns
1   teaspoon freshly ground
     green peppercorns
2   tablespoons grated
     Reggiano cheese

Cut each pita round into 8 wedges and separate the halves. Arrange on a baking sheet. Brush with the butter and sprinkle with the paprika, pepper and cheese.

Bake at 350 degrees for 12 to 15 minutes or until golden brown and crisp. Store in an airtight container.

Rosemary-Studded Quail with Fig Chanterelle Wild Rice Stuffing   serves ten

rosemary marinade

1   tablespoon chopped
     fresh rosemary
2   tablespoons orange juice
2   tablespoons spicy brown mustard
1   teaspoon freshly ground
     green peppercorns
1/2 cup walnut oil
20   Georgia mountain boneless quail

stuffed quail

1/4 cup finely chopped shallots
2   tablespoons chopped fresh parsley
1/2 cup coarsely chopped chanterelle
     mushrooms
•   butter
2   cups cooked corn bread
1   cup cooked wild rice
1/4 cup chopped figs
1   cup chicken broth
•   salt and pepper to taste

To marinate the quail, combine the rosemary, orange juice, mustard and pepper in a large bowl and mix well. Whisk in the walnut oil.

Add the quail to the marinade. Marinate in the refrigerator for 8 hours or longer.

For the stuffed quail, sauté the shallots, parsley and chanterelles in a small amount of butter in a small skillet. Combine with the corn bread, wild rice, figs, chicken broth, salt and pepper in a bowl and mix well.

Stuff the rice mixture into the quail. Place on a rack in a roasting pan. Roast at 400 degrees for 25 minutes or until golden brown. Serve with Orange and Port Gastrique (page 161).

Orange and Port Gastrique

serves ten

ingredients

1   cup port
1   cup orange juice
2   teaspoons grated orange zest
2   cups chicken demi-glace
1/4 teaspoon pepper
•   cornstarch (optional)
2   tablespoons chopped chives

Combine the wine and orange juice in a saucepan. Cook until reduced by 1/2. Add the orange zest, chicken demi-glace and pepper. Cook until reduced by 1/4.

To thicken the mixture if necessary, blend a small amount of cornstarch with enough water to make a smooth paste. Stir into the saucepan and cook until thick enough to coat the back of the spoon, stirring constantly. Stir in the chives and serve with the Rosemary-Studded Quail (page 160).

Asian Duck and Soba Noodle Salad

serves ten

soy marinade

2   cups soy sauce
3   tablespoons lime juice
3   tablespoons honey
3   tablespoons sherry
3   tablespoons sesame oil
1   tablespoon garlic chili sauce
2   teaspoons crushed gingerroot
1/4 teaspoon finely chopped cilantro
2   jalapeño peppers, sliced

salad

8   (6- to 8-ounce) duck breasts
24   ounces soba noodles
1   head Napa cabbage, julienned
1   red onion, sliced
1   pound whole snow peas, blanched
2   yellow tomatoes, chopped
2   red bell peppers, chopped
•   leaves of 1/4 bunch cilantro
•   Lemon Grass Vinaigrette
     (page 163)

garnish

•   cilantro
•   brunoise of red bell pepper

For the marinade, combine the soy sauce, lime juice, honey, sherry, sesame oil, garlic chili sauce, gingerroot, cilantro and jalapeño peppers in a bowl and whisk until well mixed.

For the salad, add the duck to the marinade. Marinate in the refrigerator for 1 or 2 days; drain.

Place the duck in a roasting pan. Roast at 425 degrees for 20 minutes. Remove to a plate and chill in the refrigerator.

Cook the noodles using the package directions. Chill in the refrigerator.

Combine the cabbage, onion, snow peas, tomatoes, bell peppers and cilantro in a bowl. Add the noodles and mix well. Slice the duck diagonally and add to the salad. Add the Lemon Grass Vinaigrette and toss lightly.

Spoon onto serving plates and garnish with cilantro and a brunoise of red bell pepper.

Lemon Grass Vinaigrette

makes two cups

ingredients

3   tablespoons light soy sauce
2   tablespoons catsup
2   tablespoons rice wine vinegar
1   teaspoon finely chopped garlic
1   teaspoon finely chopped
    gingerroot
2   teaspoons finely chopped lemon
    grass, white portion only
2   teaspoons sesame seeds, toasted
1   bunch cilantro, finely chopped
1   jalapeño pepper, finely chopped
•   salt and pepper to taste
3/4 cup canola oil

Combine the soy sauce, catsup, vinegar, garlic, gingerroot, lemon grass, sesame seeds, cilantro, jalapeño pepper, salt and pepper in a bowl and mix well. Add the canola oil gradually, mixing well.

Lobster and Asparagus Risotto Cakes

serves ten

ingredients

7	cups clam juice
2	tablespoons chopped garlic
I	cup finely chopped Vidalia onion
3	cups uncooked arborio rice
1/4	cup olive oil
3	tablespoons butter
I	cup white wine
I	cup cooked lobster
I	cup chopped asparagus
I	cup shredded mozzarella cheese
•	flour
•	olive oil

Bring the clam juice to a simmer in a saucepan over medium heat and keep warm. Sauté the garlic, onion and rice in 1/4 cup olive oil and butter in a heavy saucepan over medium-high heat for 3 minutes. Add the clam juice and wine 2 cups at a time, cooking until the liquid has been absorbed after each addition, a total of 15 to 20 minutes.

Add the lobster, asparagus and cheese. Cook for 2 to 3 minutes longer, stirring to mix the cheese as it melts.

Spread on a baking sheet and chill in the refrigerator. Cut into ten 3-inch circles with a cookie cutter. Coat each circle lightly with flour.

Sauté in a small amount of olive oil in a skillet for 2 minutes on each side or until golden brown. Serve with Pomodoro Sauce (below).

Pomodoro Sauce

serves ten

ingredients

1/2	cup thinly sliced garlic
1/4	cup extra-virgin olive oil
3	cups chopped plum tomatoes
I	teaspoon sugar
1/2	tablespoon crushed red pepper
1/4	cup julienned basil
•	salt and pepper to taste

Sauté the garlic in the olive oil in a small saucepan over medium-high heat just until the garlic begins to brown. Add the tomatoes, sugar and red pepper. Cook for 25 minutes or until reduced by 1/4, stirring occasionally. Remove from the heat and add the basil, salt and pepper.

White Chocolate Grand Marnier Torte

ingredients

2	cups finely ground shortbread cookie crumbs
1	cup finely chopped macadamias
1/2	cup melted butter
1/4	cup unflavored gelatin
1/2	cup Grand Marnier
2	vanilla beans, split
1	cup sugar
2	tablespoons grated orange zest
2	quarts heavy cream
1	cup chopped white chocolate
6	egg yolks
2	tablespoons cornstarch

Combine the cookie crumbs, macadamias and melted butter in a bowl and mix well. Press into 2 tart pans.

Soften the gelatin in the Grand Marnier in a saucepan. Add the vanilla beans, sugar and orange zest and bring to a boil, stirring to dissolve the gelatin completely.

Add the cream and return to a boil. Add the white chocolate and cook for 2 minutes, stirring to mix the chocolate as it melts.

Whisk the egg yolks and cornstarch in a small bowl. Stir a small amount of the hot mixture into the egg mixture; stir the egg mixture into the hot liquid. Bring to a simmer and cook until thickened, stirring constantly.

Strain the mixture through a fine cloth. Spoon into the prepared tart pans. Chill for 8 hours or longer. Cut into wedges with a knife rinsed with hot water.

OUTDOOR OVERTURES
DINING AL FRESCO

the menus

Stellar Suite
Chastain Concert
Picnic Nocturne

the music

Holst: *The Planets*
Telarc CD-80466

Dvořák: Slavonic Dances
Telarc CD-80497

Barber: Knoxville: Summer of 1915
Adagio for Strings and other works
Telarc CD-80250

STELLAR SUITE

chastain tidbit

The Atlanta Symphony Orchestra's Chastain Park Concerts have long been Atlanta's most popular summer entertainment, with tables in great demand. Dining al fresco, many patrons use their finest linens and silver candelabras. Years ago the Symphony Associates provided refreshments for featured artists, and one evening as I delivered the wine and fruit, a famous singer insisted on a silver goblet. Enlisting the assistance of Atlanta Symphony Orchestra Board Chair Betty Fuller, we wandered from table to table and finally secured one with the plea, "Please let us borrow this or we may not have a concert tonight!"

Anne Lester
Atlanta Symphony Associates President
  1979–1980

GARDEN *wraps* WITH GRILLED *chicken tenders* AND *grilled shrimp*

TOMATO *chutney*

LEBANESE *tabouli*

chocolate WOW COOKIES

pecan TARTS

assorted chilled imported beers
french vouvray

Grilled Chicken Tenders

serves six

ingredients

1/4	cup sherry
1/2	cup teriyaki sauce
1/2	cup reduced-sodium soy sauce
1/4	cup dark sesame oil
1	teaspoon minced gingerroot
2	tablespoons sesame seeds
2	pounds chicken tenders or sliced breasts

Combine the sherry, teriyaki sauce, soy sauce, sesame oil, gingerroot and sesame seeds in a bowl and mix well.

Add the chicken tenders and marinate, covered, in the refrigerator for 6 hours or longer.

Drain the chicken and thread onto skewers. Grill over hot coals for 4 minutes on each side or until cooked through.

Note: *To present your stellar suite picnic, serve the grilled chicken tenders and grilled shrimp (page 170) as wraps. Place them on large leaves of leaf lettuce and top with julienned jicama, sliced carrot, mint leaves, sliced green onions and cucumber slices. Drizzle with fresh lime juice and wrap in the lettuce leaf to enclose the filling. The tabouli (page 173) can be served in the same manner.*

Garden Wraps with Grilled Chicken Tenders on page 169 and Grilled Shrimp

Grilled Shrimp

ingredients

4   garlic cloves, minced
3   tablespoons finely chopped
    fresh basil
1/4   cup finely chopped fresh parsley
2   tablespoons finely chopped fresh
    cilantro
1/2   cup lemon juice or lime juice
3/4   cup vegetable oil
1/2   cup reduced-sodium soy sauce
1/3   cup chopped onion
2   teaspoons pepper, or to taste
2   pounds peeled shrimp, deveined

Combine the garlic with half the basil, parsley and cilantro in a mortar. Grind with a pestle to mix well.

Combine the remaining basil, parsley and cilantro with the lemon juice, oil, soy sauce, onion and pepper in a small bowl. Stir in the crushed garlic mixture.

Combine with the shrimp in a large bowl and mix to coat well. Marinate, covered, in the refrigerator for 8 hours or longer.

Drain the shrimp and thread onto skewers. Grill over hot coals for 5 minutes on each side or until opaque.

Note: *To present your stellar suite picnic, serve the grilled chicken tenders (page 169) and grilled shrimp as wraps. Place them on large leaves of leaf lettuce and top with julienned jicama, sliced carrot, mint leaves, sliced green onions and cucumber slices. Drizzle with fresh lime juice and wrap in the lettuce leaf to enclose the filling. The tabouli (page 173) can be served in the same manner.*

Tomato Chutney

ingredients

1	lemon
5	cups chopped unpeeled tomatoes, about 6 tomatoes
2	cups chopped peeled tart apples
2	cups chopped onions
1	(8-ounce) package pitted dates, cut into thirds
4	large garlic cloves, minced
•	juice of 1 lemon
3/4	cup tomato juice
3/4	cup apple juice
3/4	cup cider vinegar
1/2	cup honey
2	teaspoons ground coriander
1	teaspoon salt or salt substitute
•	cayenne pepper to taste
1 1/2	teaspoons black pepper

Allow the ingredients in the chutney to blend and marry before serving for the best flavor. The cayenne may seem somewhat spicy at first, but the flavor will mellow.

Cut the unpeeled lemon into paper-thin slices; cut the slices into quarters. Combine with the tomatoes, apples, onions, dates and garlic in a 6-quart saucepan.

Add the lemon juice, tomato juice, apple juice, vinegar, honey, coriander, salt, cayenne pepper and black pepper and mix well. Bring to a boil and turn down the heat. Simmer for 30 minutes, stirring occasionally.

Cool the mixture in the saucepan. Spoon into clean jars or freezer containers. Store in the refrigerator or freezer until needed.

Serve with meat dishes or as a baste for pork, chicken or fish. It is also good on toast.

Lebanese Tabouli

ingredients

3/4   cup (No.1 size) cracked wheat
2   or 3 bunches parsley,
       finely chopped
1   bunch green onions with tops,
       finely chopped
5   or 6 Roma tomatoes, finely
       chopped, or 3 tomatoes, seeded,
       finely chopped
1   bunch mint, chopped, or
       1 tablespoon dried mint
•   juice of 2 or 3 lemons
3/4   cup extra-virgin olive oil
1   tablespoon lemon pepper

This Lebanese dish is excellent in the summer when tomatoes and fresh mint are available from the garden. The cracked wheat can be found at specialty or Middle Eastern markets.

Rinse the cracked wheat in a strainer; drain and press out the water.

Combine the parsley, green onions, tomatoes and mint in a large bowl. Add the wheat and toss to mix well. Add the lemon juice, olive oil and lemon pepper and toss again.

Chill for 1 hour or longer before serving. Wrap in lettuce leaves to serve at a picnic.

Chocolate Wow Cookies

makes two and one-half dozen

ingredients

$1/2$ cup butter
6 ounces semisweet chocolate
2 eggs
$3/4$ cup sugar
$1/3$ cup flour
1 teaspoon baking powder
$1/4$ cup baking cocoa
$1^1/2$ teaspoons vanilla extract
$1/4$ teaspoon salt
2 cups pecans, coarsely ground
6 ounces semisweet chocolate chips

Melt the butter in a small saucepan over low heat. Add the chocolate and cook until melted, stirring to blend well.

Beat the eggs and sugar in a mixing bowl at high speed for 2 minutes or until thickened and pale yellow. Reduce the mixer speed to medium and beat in the chocolate mixture.

Add the flour, baking powder, baking cocoa, vanilla and salt; beat for 2 minutes. Stir in the pecans and chocolate chips.

Drop by $1/2$ teaspoonfuls onto a greased cookie sheet and press to flatten slightly. Bake at 350 degrees for 6 to 8 minutes or just until set. Cool on the cookie sheet for several minutes; remove to a wire rack to cool completely.

Pecan Tarts

makes two dozen

ingredients

$1/2$ cup butter, softened
$1/2$ cup sugar
2 egg yolks
2 cups sifted flour
1 teaspoon almond extract
$1/2$ cup margarine or butter
$1/3$ cup dark corn syrup
1 cup confectioners' sugar
1 cup chopped pecans
• pecan halves (optional)

Cream the butter and sugar in a mixing bowl until light and fluffy. Add the egg yolks, flour and almond extract and mix well. Press into miniature tart shells or $1^3/4$-inch muffin cups.

Bake at 400 degrees for 8 to 10 minutes.

Combine the margarine, corn syrup and confectioners' sugar in a saucepan and bring to a boil. Stir in the chopped pecans. Spoon into the prepared tart shells. Top with a pecan half if desired.

Bake at 350 degrees for 5 minutes. Cool in the tart shells before removing.

Chocolate Wow Cookies

CHASTAIN CONCERT

sometimes it's the pits

For a ballet or opera, orchestras play in a "pit," which is not a very glamorous name. In fact, some pits are literally pits. I once played at a community center where the pit was totally concrete, including the stage which overhung half of it. Cyclone fencing stretched from the stage to the top of the pit to keep people from falling in. We were basically caged animals!

Bruce Kenney, Horn

papa doble

carrot STICKS

asparagus BUNDLES TIED WITH GREEN ONIONS

salmon BURGERS

DILL *bread*

GARLIC *pickles*

MANGO *marmalade*

white french table wine

FRENCH *lemon cake*

FRESH *strawberries*

Papa Doble

ingredients

5   ounces white rum
6   ounces spiced rum
•   juice of 1 lime
•   pineapple juice
•   orange juice
•   grapefruit juice
•   maraschino cherry juice

For the best flavor, the juices in this drink should be chilled before preparing. Adjust the amounts of juice to suit your taste.

Combine the white rum, spiced rum, lime juice, pineapple juice, orange juice, grapefruit juice and cherry juice in a blender container and process until smooth.

Carrot Sticks

serves four

ingredients

4   carrots
2   teaspoons kosher salt
2   limes, cut into 8 wedges

Scrape the carrots and cut into sticks. Arrange in a fan on a serving plate. Place the salt in a small bowl and place at the base of the fan. Add the lime wedges. To serve, squeeze the lime juice over the carrots and sprinkle with the salt.

Salmon Burgers

ingredients

1	pound boneless salmon fillet, chopped
1/4	cup finely chopped red onion
1/4	cup finely chopped red bell pepper
1/2	teaspoon Worcestershire sauce
1/4	teaspoon hot pepper sauce (optional)
1	tablespoon minced fresh basil plus 2 tablespoons shredded fresh basil
•	salt and freshly ground pepper to taste
1	large egg
1/4	cup fresh fine bread crumbs

garnish

- lemon wedges

Combine the salmon, onion, bell pepper, Worcestershire sauce, pepper sauce, basil, salt and pepper in a bowl and mix well. Add the egg and bread crumbs and mix well.

Shape into 4 patties. Grill, broil or fry until golden brown and cooked through. Garnish servings with lemon wedges.

Dill Bread

ingredients

1	envelope dry yeast
1/4	cup lukewarm water
1	cup cottage cheese
2	tablespoons sugar
1	tablespoon minced onion
1	egg
1	tablespoon butter, softened
1/4	teaspoon baking soda
2	teaspoons dillseeds
1	teaspoon dillweed
1	teaspoon salt
2 1/4 to 2 1/2	cups flour

Dissolve the yeast in the lukewarm water. Combine the cottage cheese, sugar, onion, egg, butter, baking soda, dillseeds, dillweed and salt in a large bowl. Add the yeast mixture and mix well. Add enough flour to form a stiff dough and mix well.

Let rise, covered, in a warm place until doubled in bulk. Punch down and place in a greased loaf pan. Let rise until doubled in bulk.

Bake at 350 degrees for 45 to 60 minutes or until golden brown. Remove to a wire rack to cool.

Mango Marmalade

ingredients

9	ounces coarsely chopped prepared mango chutney
10	ounces orange marmalade
1	large mango, chopped
1/4	cup hot spicy grainy mustard
1	tablespoon prepared horseradish
•	juice of 1 lemon

Combine the mango chutney, orange marmalade, mango, mustard, horseradish and lemon juice in a medium bowl and mix well.

Store in an airtight container in the refrigerator. Serve with grilled meats, chicken or fish, or with meat loaf.

Garlic Pickles

ingredients

6	to 8 pickling cucumbers
1/4	cup canning and pickling salt
1	tablespoon mustard seeds
1	tablespoon dried dillweed, or 2 tablespoons fresh dillweed
1	tablespoon sugar
4	large garlic cloves, thinly sliced
2	whole cloves
1	teaspoon whole peppercorns
1	teaspoon turmeric
1	cup distilled white vinegar
1/2	cup water

Adjust the ingredients in this recipe to suit individual tastes. For the crispest pickles, use canning and pickling salt. Table salt will reduce the crunch and color of pickles.

Cut the cucumbers into quarters lengthwise. Toss with the salt in a nonmetal container. Let stand for 30 minutes, stirring occasionally. Rinse in a colander under cold water.

Combine the mustard seeds, dillweed, sugar, garlic, cloves, peppercorns and turmeric in a 1-quart jar and mix well. Pack the cucumbers in the jar. Pour a mixture of the vinegar and water into the jar and shake to mix well.

Chill in the refrigerator for 2 days or longer; 7 days is recommended.

French Lemon Cake

serves eight

ingredients

1	lemon
1/2	cup sugar
1/2	cup unsalted butter or margarine, cut into 4 pieces
2	large eggs
1	cup minus 2 tablespoons flour
1	teaspoon baking powder
1/2	cup confectioners' sugar

garnish

- confectioners' sugar

Peel just the yellow zest from the lemon; reserve the lemon and place the zest in the food processor. Add the sugar gradually, processing for 20 seconds. Add the butter 1 piece at a time, processing until mixed. Add the eggs 1 at a time, processing for 15 to 20 seconds after each addition.

Mix the flour and baking powder together. Add to the food processor and pulse just until the flour is mixed; do not overmix.

Spoon into a buttered and floured 8-inch cake pan. Bake at 350 degrees for 25 minutes or until light golden brown. Cool in the pan for 10 minutes; remove to a wire rack.

Squeeze the juice from the reserved lemon into a bowl and stir in 1/2 cup confectioners' sugar. Spoon over the warm cake and let stand until cool. Garnish with additional confectioners' sugar. Store, covered, in the refrigerator.

for six
PICNIC NOCTURNE

shared memories

When I first volunteered for the Women's Committee in the 1950s, it had an informal structure and indefinite membership. By the mid-1960s the structure had formalized, with the Women's Committee, Junior Committee, and the Suburban Committees merging into The Women's Association. By the 1980s and the addition of male members, the name changed to the Atlanta Symphony Associates.

Margaret Hall
Atlanta Symphony Associates President
    1970–1971

In the mid-1960s the Atlanta Symphony Orchestra moved from the 5,000-seat Municipal Auditorium to the new 1,760-seat Symphony Hall. More than a hundred volunteers assisted in quickly rescheduling 30,000 young people for the smaller facility.

Barbara Wylly
Atlanta Symphony Associates President
    1975–1976

cheese AND *fruit tray*

YELLOW TOMATO *shrimp gazpacho*

hanna sauvignon blanc

ROSEMARY ORANGE *pork tenderloin*

PEARL *couscous with* GRILLED *vegetables*

seghesia red zinfandel OR

estancia pinot noir

BLUEBERRY *coconut pie*

pommerey brut champagne

FROM *Carole Parks Catering*

Yellow Tomato Shrimp Gazpacho

serves six

ingredients

1   tablespoon grapeseed oil
2   tablespoons chopped
     fresh tarragon
•   salt and pepper to taste
24 large (26- to 30-count) shrimp,
     peeled, deveined
3   yellow tomatoes, seeded, chopped
1/2 red bell pepper, seeded, chopped
2   cucumbers, peeled, seeded,
     chopped
1/2 red onion, chopped
1   mango, chopped
1/4 cup rice wine vinegar
1/4 cup clam juice
2   tablespoons lemon juice
1/4 cup grapeseed oil
2   tablespoons frozen orange juice
     concentrate, thawed
2   tablespoons chopped
     fresh tarragon

Combine 1 tablespoon grapeseed oil, 2 tablespoons tarragon, salt and pepper in a bowl and mix well. Add the shrimp. Marinate, covered, in the refrigerator for 20 minutes; drain. Grill the shrimp over hot coals for 3 minutes on each side or until opaque. Chill in the refrigerator.

Combine the yellow tomatoes, bell pepper, cucumbers, onion and mango in a bowl. Add the vinegar, clam juice, lemon juice, 1/4 cup grapeseed oil, orange juice concentrate and 2 tablespoons tarragon and mix well. Stir in the shrimp.

Chill the mixture for 4 hours or longer. Spoon onto a bed of lettuce to serve.

Rosemary Orange Pork Tenderloin

serves six

ingredients

1   (12-ounce) can frozen orange
    juice concentrate, thawed
1/2 cup dry sherry
1/4 cup soy sauce
2   tablespoons hot pepper sauce
1/3 cup honey Dijon mustard
1   tablespoon chopped garlic
2   tablespoons finely chopped
    fresh rosemary
3   pounds pork tenderloin

The marinade in this recipe can also be used for chicken.

Combine the orange juice concentrate, sherry, soy sauce, pepper sauce, mustard, garlic and rosemary in a bowl and mix well. Add the pork and turn to coat well. Marinate in the refrigerator for 2 to 6 hours.

Drain the pork and insert a meat thermometer. Grill over hot coals for 7 minutes on each side or until the meat thermometer registers medium. Cool the pork and chill until serving time. Slice to serve.

Pearl Couscous with Grilled Vegetables

serves six

ingredients

•   vegetables, such as asparagus,
    tomatoes, yellow squash, red and
    yellow bell peppers, eggplant
    and/or red onions
•   olive oil
•   fresh herbs
•   salt and pepper to taste
2   cups uncooked couscous
•   saffron to taste
3   cups chicken broth
1 1/4 cups chopped fresh dill
2   tablespoons lemon juice
1/4 cup grated Parmesan cheese

Cut the vegetables into large pieces. Brush with olive oil and sprinkle with fresh herbs, salt and pepper. Grill until tender and cool to room temperature.

Cook the couscous with a pinch of saffron in the chicken broth in a saucepan for 20 minutes; cool. Add the vegetables, dill, lemon juice and Parmesan cheese and mix well.

Blueberry Coconut Pie

serves six

ingredients

2   quarts fresh or frozen blueberries
2   tablespoons cornstarch
•   juice and grated zest of 2 limes
1   (9-inch) pie shell
1/2 cup flour
1/2 cup sugar
3   tablespoons butter
1/3 cup coconut

Combine the blueberries, cornstarch, lime juice and lime zest in a bowl and toss to mix well. Spoon into the pie shell.

Combine the flour, sugar, butter and coconut in a bowl and mix until crumbly. Sprinkle over the blueberry mixture.

Bake at 350 degrees for 30 to 45 minutes or until golden brown. Serve with whipped cream or ice cream.

Recipe Contributors

Sharing their secrets of fine entertaining and dining are the following recipe contributors:

Jane Ackerman
Dot Adams
Margaret Allen
Lu Allgood
Nancy Anderson
Jeanine Andrews
Betty Arden
Marion Atkins
Molham Awadalla
Joy Hafner Bailey
C. F. Bakker
Christine Beard
Diane Benetar
Ginger Beverly
Verna Black
Joan Blankenship
Juliette Bowman
Eleanor Bradshore
Margaret Bruce
Bette Buddin
Francis Bunzl
Nita Burge
Harriet Burks
Rosemary Buttermore
JoAn Chace
Jay Christie
Caroline Coburn
Susan Connell
Janis Coovert
Honey Corbin
Sandy Cotterman
Vella Cowan
Nancy Cox
Peggy Dalbey

Frank Dans
Nancy Dawson
Rina Delaplane
Monice Demoulin
Lauri Dick
Brenda Dunn
Marcia Epstein
Elizabeth Etoll
Kathy Evans
Carla Fackler
Beth Feiner
Molly Feldman
Al Finfer
Penny Finfer
Lisa Freschi
Sally Gayer
Irene Walker Gerson
Francis Gould
Mary Gramling
Bobbie Green
Jola Greiner
Emily Gyann
Margaret Hall
Barbara Halpern
Gale Harman
Sue Harris
Debbie Hattox
Celia Hauschild
Ella Herlihy
Millie Hix
Carolyn Hockman
Doris Hoenig
Bobbie Holman
Pat Holmes

Emily Hubbard
Judy Hutton
Barbara Jennings
Denny Jewart
Brenda Peace Joiner
Laura Kearney
Eva Kelly
Anne Kennedy
Marion Kent
Mary Kitchens
Dona Klein
Rose Mary Kolpatzki
Helen Kotsher
Mary Kraft
Trina Topshe Kriss
Marcy Lamberson
Tracy Lamport
Joanne Lecraw
Lucy Lee
Amy Leventhal
Liz Levine
Jun-Cheng Lin
Susan Lipsky
Eftichia Macris
Nan Maddox
Judy Marks
Adair Massey
Carolyn McAfee
Eunice McAleer
Pam McAllister
Liz McClure
Elizabeth McDonald
Lockey Allen McDonald
Martha McElhannon

Cindy McGowan
Betty McKemie
Marcy McTier
Molly Mednikow
Patty Meyer
Jeanne Mileur
Nicole Miller
Heidi Nitchie
Stacey Tappis Offer
Tamara Ogden
Virginia O'Leary
Jackie Owings
Jason Peck
Stella Perzik
Doris Pidgeon
Mary Pless
Janice Podber
Mercy Ponce de Leor
Amy Porter
Helen Porter
Yvonne Powers
Suzanne Press
Lucia Pulgram
Gail Rader
Carolyn Randall
Heidi Rice
Faith Richardson
Betty Roesel
Lynne Rourke
Amy Rubin
John Rubin
Leslie Schaitberger
Rudy Schlegel
Judy Schmidt

Recipe Testers

Our recipe testers gave their time and financial support to ensure the highest quality possible.

Kim Scholes
Essie Schorr
Carol Sharkey
Melinda Sharp
Suzanne Shull
Charles Siegel, Jr.
Sharon Silvermintz
Christina Smith
Lessie Smithgall
Rochelle Smoleck
Elizabeth Morgan Spiegel
Staci Stager
Helen Stanley
Susan Staples
Pat Stowell
Sue Strelecki
Nancy Taffel
Fareba Beyani Teimorabadi
Peter Teimorabadi
Mary Ellen Thatcher
Kiki Thomas
Kathleen Tice

Mary Tierney
Sarah Belle Tollison
Josephine Topshe
Margaret Towers
Shirley Trapp
Joyce Troutman
Nina Tucker
Joan Turcotte
Gail Vrana
Thelma Waldman
Sherry Warner
Suzy Wasserman
Nancy Waterfill
Jennifer Webster
Patti Wheeler
Edward White
Penny Whittington
Sue Williams
Mary Wilson
Richard Wise
Dottie Zaworsky

We hope that we have not inadvertently excluded anyone from this list. We deeply regret that we were unable to include all of the wonderful recipes that were submitted, due to availability of space.

Restaurant and Caterer Contributors

Affairs to Remember
Bacchanalia
Carole Parks Catering
Horseradish Grill

Legendary Events
Pano's and Paul's
Seeger's

Jeanine Andrews
Norah Byrnes
Nancy Chunka
Belinda Cramer
Kathy Evans
Barbara Fields
Nancy Fields
Al Finfer
Peggy Finfer
Sally Finkelstein
Michael Fournier
Stephanie Fournier
Lisa Freschi
Dawn Gibson
Barbara Halpern
Michelle Hardner
Ella Herlihy
Anne Herman
Bea Hill
Carolyn Hockman
Diane Howard
Debra Hurst
Judy Hutton
Barbara Jennings
Mary Lamberson
Susan Lipsky
Elizabeth McDonald
Rob McDonald
Cindy McGowan

Patty Meyer
Francine Morrison
Stephanie November
Raphael Offer
Stacey Tappis Offer
Erin Olander
Jackie Owings
Sonia Picallo
Mary Pless
Adrienne Price
Yavonne Rodriguez
Amy Rubin
Jonathan Rubin
Leslie Schaitberger
Essie Schorr
Veronica Silverstein
Larry Smith, Sr.
Linda Smith
Susie Smith
Staci Stager
Sara Thaxton
Liz Troy
Barbara Ulven
Thelma Waldman
Suzy Wasserman
Melissa Woodward

Index

Sounds Delicious

Benefiting the Atlanta Symphony Orchestra

Name _____

Street Address _____

City _____ State _____ Zip _____

Phone _____

Your Order	Quantity	Total
Sounds Delicious $27.95 per book including CD		$
Case of 6 **Sounds Delicious** $150.00 per case		$
Shipping & Handling ($5.00 for first book; add $1.50 for each additional book)		$
Georgia residents add $1.96 sales tax (7%) per book		$
Total		$

[   ] Check enclosed. Please make check payable to Atlanta Symphony Associates.

[   ] Charge to: [   ] VISA   [   ] MasterCard   [   ] American Express

Account Number _____ Expiration Date _____

Cardholder Name _____

Signature _____

To order by mail, send to: Atlanta Symphony Associates
P.O. Box 79178 • Atlanta, Georgia 30357-7178 • 404-733-4963

*Proceeds benefit the fund-raising, community outreach, and educational efforts
of the Atlanta Symphony Orchestra.*

Photocopies accepted.